REBEL BEFORE HIS TIME

The Story of John Ball
and the Peasants' Revolt

by

BRIAN BIRD

The front cover illustration is by courtesy of
Tressell Publications of Brighton

REBEL BEFORE HIS TIME

The Story of John Ball and the Peasants' Revolt

by

Brian Bird

CHURCHMAN PUBLISHING :
WORTHING : 1987

REBEL BEFORE HIS TIME
The Story of John Ball and the Peasants' Revolt

by

Brian Bird

was first published in Great Britain by

Churchman Publishing Limited
117 Broomfield Avenue
Worthing
West Sussex
BN14 7SF

Publisher: Peter Smith

Represented in Kingston, Ontario, Sydney and Wellington

Distributed to the book trade by

Bailey Bros. & Swinfen Limited
Warner House
Wear Bay Road
Folkestone
Kent
CT19 6PH

ISBN 1 85093 057 0

Typeset by CPJ Fotoset Limited of Worthing
and printed by Antony Rowe Limited of Chippenham

John Ball, leader of the Peasants' Revolt of 1381 and thus one of the first champions of human rights, has generally been portrayed – in common with fellow rebel Wat Tyler – as one of history's scoundrels. Brian Bird's researches into Ball's origin and position in the church has revealed previously unknown facts about this dissident priest, and it is on this new information that he has based his controversial study.

This book will attract a far more general readership than many historical works, focusing as it does not only on the leaders of the Peasants' Revolt but filling in much of the background. It explains, for example, why the peasants became aware of their strength, how the Black Death contributed to the social unrest and how the three Poll Taxes, introduced by Richard II to finance the hundred years war, pushed the ordinary people to breaking point.

Ball's part in the Revolt is fully dealt with from the beginning of his involvement until his arrest, trial and execution. The last three chapters consider the reasons why the revolt failed, its effects and the lessons to be learned from it.

FOREWORD

FOREWORD

by D. T-D. Clarke, M.A., F.S.A.

Curator, Colchester and Essex Museum

The Peasants' Revolt of 1381 is an episode of English history which "every school boy knows", and has long been in the history book, and like most such events, has been variously evaluated according to the attitudes of subsequent historians.

Its close associations with Essex, and especially Colchester, as well as its concern for the underprivileged, have commended it to Brian Bird as a subject for intensive research; the more so since he came to Colchester, after a life of dedicated service to the Christian faith, to live but a stone's throw from where John Ball may have held property and only a few minutes walk from the church in which he may have celebrated Mass.

It has been my privilege to know Brian Bird for a considerable time, and it was on his suggestion that, on behalf of the Borough Council, the museum service erected a plaque commemorating John Ball in 1981. I therefore have pleasure in commending this book to the turbulent seas of history; for only by the writing of new studies can theories be tested and truth be more clearly ascertained.

As time passes, interpretations change: it is equally certain that the issues herein recorded do not. They are thus a deserving subject of reflection for our, and every succeeding, generation.

David T-D. Clarke

CONTENTS

AUTHOR'S NOTE

I became interested in John Ball, priest leader of the Peasants' Revolt of 1381, when I came to retire to Colchester in 1971. After several years of research, culminating in the discovery, in 1975, of the hitherto unknown facts about his origin and position in the church of St. James in the town, I felt that some book ought to be written about him and the part he played in the insurrection, incorporating the new information obtained.

I should like to express my gratitude to my American correspondent, Mrs Sandra Jane Eccli, a History Graduate of the Virginia Polytechnic and State University, engaged in writing a novel on the English Peasants' Revolt. Her frequent letters to me have contained a mine of valuable information and have, invariably, been bubbling over with enthusiasm.

I am grateful also for the help of Dr David Stephenson, a graduate of Brasenose College, Oxford, formerly Lecturer in History at the Colchester Institute of Higher Education, with whom I collaborated in a short article entitled "WHO WAS JOHN BALL?" in ESSEX ARCHAEOLOGY AND HISTORY, 1977. At one time leader of the Colchester History Research Group and author of a new History of Colchester, he has, throughout, shown unfailing interest in the development of this present work.

BRIAN BIRD

COLCHESTER, 1987

CHAPTER 1

Historical Causes of the Peasants' Revolt

THE fourteenth century in Europe may be looked upon as a watershed in its historical development. It was the great age of chivalry. The knightly code prevailed, a code based on ideals of courteous behaviour and the value of ceremonial, producing an 'espirit de corps' which knit together the ruling class of the Continent. It was halfway through this century that the noble Order of the Garter was founded by Kind Edward III in England.

But this chivalric age has been noted for two outstanding factors – the cruelty of its men and the beauty of its women. F. George Kay, in his *Lady of The Sun*,[1] a study of the life and times of Alice Ferrers, mistress of Edward III, writes:

"A delightful feature of a century of violence and cruelty is that the dark picture of perpetual war, recurrent plague and economic chaos is relieved by the grace and loveliness of its women."

It was during this period that the feudal system, so long established, reached its zenith, and began to show signs of decay. It was a system which, emerging from its preceding slave system, held sway for so many centuries that its protagonists, the nobility, had assumed that they now had some divine right to continue in their dominant position forever.

It was this arrogant assumption on the part of the great lords that contributed ultimately to their downfall. For they had a blind spot. They could not see that the serfs, villeins and peasants, who by their work contributed so much to their

---

[1] Frederick Muller, 1966.

masters' comfort, were human beings also, with feelings and rights which had to be considered. It had never entered into the heads of the aristocracy that, as a radical thinker declaimed three hundred years later, "the poorest he that is in England hath a life to live as the greatest he."[1]

So, as the century developed, and following the Black Death in 1349, conditions in Europe and, indeed, in England were ready for a change. This great chivalric age became, also, an age of profound social and political crisis such as always accompanies outmoded social systems. There were sporadic risings everywhere in Europe, foreshadowing the collapse of a decaying order of society. Conflict was now inevitable between the old feudal lords and the emerging strength of the serfs who were beginning to unite.

In Europe, from the twelfth century onwards, there was a definite feeling of solidarity among the peasant communities. Critical and heretical thinking in France, Italy, Germany and the Low Countries, with its subversive social and political implications, led to peasant rebellions which were symptomatic of the whole of the society of medieval Europe between the fourteenth and sixteenth centuries.

These early fourteenth century heretical-social movements were known by the general name of the Cathari, from the Greek 'katharoi' meaning 'pure'. They included such groups in France as the Shepherds or Pastoreux (reported on by the contemporary English chronicler, Matthew Paris), the Albigensians, and Waldensians, who preached apostolic Christianity, and the revolutionary "spiritual" Franciscans in Italy. Here also flourished the Apolistic Brethren, or Apostles, with their strong millenarian teaching.

In maritime Flanders, a revolt between 1323–1377 led to the peasants taking over the organisation of the whole area. And later, in 1380/1381, (almost coincident with the English Peasants' Revolt) there were risings in France and the Flemish towns under the famous Ghent leader, Philip Van Artevelde.

The Tuchin movement in central France between 1360 and 1400 was a revolt that was perhaps unique in one respect in that

---

[1] Gerrard Winstanley, 1649.

2

it led to the development of social banditry, small bands working effectively along modern guerilla-style lines.

But the revolt which was perhaps most like the situation in England was that of the "Jacquerie" in the Paris region in 1358. Under their leader, Guillaume Câle, the French peasants and workers, living in misery, rose up against a discredited nobility. The conditions of the people had been further worsened by the bands of hired English and French soldiers who were living off the countryside.

This revolt of the "Jacques Bonhomme" (John Goodman) of France was the shortest and worst organised of continental revolts. Although supported by some nobles, who sympathised with the plight of the peasants, the rebels only succeeded in destroying the records of their obligations before they were defeated when their leader was treacherously murdered by a trick identical to that employed twenty-one years later against English peasant leader, Wat Tyler.

Describing the "Jacquerie" rising, French chronicler, Jean Froissart, wrote:

> "One of them got up and said that the nobility of France, knights and squires, were disgracing and betraying the realm, and that it would be a good thing if they were all destroyed. At this time they all shouted 'He is right! He is right! Shame on any man who saves the gentry from being wiped out!'"

Chronicler Jean de Venette, adds the following comment on the situation:

> "The peasants, seeing that the nobles gave them no protection, but rather oppressed them as heavily as the enemy, rose and took arms against the Nobles of France.
> . . . The number of peasants eager to extirpate the nobles and their wives and to destroy their manor houses, grew until it was estimated at five thousand."[1]

Some of the most serious of these mass movements of the workers were undoubtedly caused by the actions of the nobles and landlords themselves. In attempting to stem the rising aspirations of their serfs, they took repressive measures which

---

[1] Chronicle, Ed. J. Birdsall and R. A. Newhall, p. 76.

upset the customary relationships which had existed for generations. Normal expectations of the peasants were being disappointed, and there was developing among them a strong sense of frustration.

The medieval division of society into the nobles who fought for all, the churchmen who prayed for all, and the peasants who worked for all, had been established for centuries. The existing social hierarchy was thought of as an earthly reflection of a heavenly order, with the king as the head, the nobility as the hands, religion as the soul, and the peasants as the feet of the whole body. Man's tendency to create God in his own image and then to assume that the reverse was the case, was clearly shown in medieval views of society.

All this was now being challenged by the peasants, serfs and villeins. They felt they were no longer prepared to accept the role of being the feet of the body politic, expected to plod away, year in and year out, working for the good of the whole and sharing none of its benefits. The workers were beginning to develop a definite class consciousness, and this, incidentally, almost five hundred years before such an idea was promulgated in England by a German Jewish political thinker.

Revolutionary poems and songs were now circulating freely throughout England and Europe. Socially subversive writings such as "The Robin Hood Ballads", "The Tales of Gamelin", and William Langland's "Vision of Piers Plowman" were becoming known and understood. One jingle in particular became the watchword for revolt and spread across the Continent. It contained the words:–

"When Adam delved and Eve Span,
Who was then the gentleman?"

This fourteenth century folk lyric, which English Peasants' Revolt leader, the priest, John Ball, used effectively in his preaching, can be traced, in its earliest source, to the school of English revolutionary poet, Richard Rolle, about 1340. The original version reads:–

"When Adam delved and Eva spun,
Say, if you will know,
The pride of man had not begun,
That now lays him low."

A common traditional version was shortened to:–
"When Adam delved and Eva span,
Where was then the pride of man?"
A German version dates from the German Peasants' War of the sixteenth century, and was circulating in East Prussia in 1525, as follows:–
"Do Adam rent und Eva span,
Wo war do der Edelman?
Im Kustal war Er . . ."
The translation of the last line reads significantly – "He was in the cowshed"!

Prophets of doom there were in abundance. There was no shortage of men of vision who foresaw the collapes of the existing unjust system, especially in England. Richard Rolle de Hampole (1290–1349) born at Thornton in Yorkshire, was a mystic and ascetic who saw this clearly. He protested against it in his simple ethical teaching and was critical of many of the conventional views of his contemporary religion.

Lawrence Minot (1300–1352), lyric poet and soldierly minstrel, with his alliterative measure reflected clearly the popular feelings of the day, embodying, in a most vivid way, the militant England of the period.

Poet John Gower (1325–1408) an esquire of Kent with manors in Norfolk and Suffolk, wrote of the Peasant rising in Kent with obvious personal knowledge. In his *Mirour de l'Omme,* published in 1375, he wrote gloomily that "the world goeth fast from bad to worse", and made the ominous forecast that "three things, all of the same sort, are merciless when they get the upper hand; – a water flood, a wasting fire, and the common multitude of small folk". In one of his poems, written between 1376 and 1378, he foresaw accurately the forthcoming Peasants' Revolt of 1381.

Faced with all this, the common folk found consolation in the growing realisation that things were not fore-ordained to remain as they were. The doctrine of a primary egalitarian State of Nature was familiar both in Europe and England. Men began to see that this Golden Age was not irretrievably lost in the distant past. It could come into being quite soon. The Day of Judgement was nearer than many people imagined.

In the *Dialogue of Dives and Pauper*, an early fourteenth century writing, we read:–

"By the law of kynde [Nature] and by Goddess Love, all thynge is common."

In the Fifth Epistle of Clement, and the works of St. Ambrose, such exhortations as follows were made:

"In commune to all, rich and poore, the earth was made. Why will ye ritch chalenge proper right herein? Kinde knoweth no riches, that bringeth forth al men poore."

This fantasy of an Egalitarian State of Nature had never previously acted as a dynamic social myth. But, reinforced by social criticism of a more personal and passionate kind, it began to prove effective. It came to a head in the turbulent years around 1380, and found its expression in the preaching of many of the humble working clergy.

CHAPTER 2

The Role of the Church

BECAUSE of the vast wealth it had accumulated, the Medieval Church was the main bulwark of the feudal order of Society in Europe, and, as the forces of social change began to develop, the common people found themselves more and more in conflict with it. Various Popes fulminated against the Cathari groups, and authorised the ruling classes to proceed against them with fire and sword. In the thirteenth century, the Inquisition was set up to assist with this, excommunicating heretics, and then handing them over to the secular authorities to be put to death.

Wherever any heretical movement began to assume any dangerous dimensions, it was ruthlessly persecuted by both Church and State, for both authorities realised that any such movement threatened not merely the authority of the Church, but the whole structure of their day.

The Inquisition assumed its most cruel and effective form in France and Spain. In Germany, its activities were only sporadic, and in England it was unable to obtain any foothold. It was by means of such bloody violence that the Medieval Church dealth with heresies which threatened its position in society, and, indeed, the very foundations of that society.

Writing of these movements, Church historian, Dollinger, says of them:–

> "Every heretical doctrine which arose in the Middle Ages had explicit or implicitly a revolutionary character. Those Gnostic sects, the Cathari and the Albigenses, which specially provoked the harsh and ruthless legislation of the Middle Ages and had to be put down in a series of bloody struggles, were the Socialists and

Communists of that time. They attacked marriage, the family and property."

So, by and large, we find this unholy alliance of Church and State, to be a dominant feature in this period. Their interests were in common. Both were large landowners, both owned many serfs, and both exploited them. In actual fact, the most efficient and ruthless landlords were the great monasteries, whose priors and abbots were often more severe to their serfs than were the secular lords and nobles.

As the emergent peasant class began to realise its strength, it found ranged against it, that powerful combination of the rulers of its society and the hierarchy of its Church, standing solidly together in the understanding that any attack on one or other of them was an attack on both.

That the hierarchy of the Church throughout Europe was on the side of the nobility was not surprising since most of the leaders of the Church, the cardinals, bishops, abbots and priors, came themselves from the ruling class. In fact, the' prelates were statesmen and the statesmen prelates. Men held, simultaneously, high offices of both Church and State. There was no fundamental conflict of interest.

And, even where we find Church reformers such as John Wycliffe in England, and, later, Martin Luther in Germany, attacking the Church, they were both quick to condemn the rising of the peasants which followed, as a natural consequence, from their teaching. For they both realised, too late perhaps, that a policy of disrespect for the Eucharist could easily lead to a similar disrespect for all law and authority. As a contemporary writer put it – "Those whose learning could dethrone a Pope, might one day dethrone a king!" So, when the crunch came and the peasants rose both in England and Germany, these two erstwhile reformers drew in their horns and disassociated themselves from the fury they were partly responsible for causing, Wycliffe retiring to his studies in his country rectory at Lutterworth, and Luther to domestic joys with his beloved ex-nun, Catherine.

The late Bishop Gore, of Oxford, one of the most learned of English bishops, once pointed out that, when Christianity became the official religion of the Roman Empire under

Constantine in 313 AD, it lost nine-tenths of its moral fibre and vitality. Forgotten was the example of the Apostolic Church, with its teaching of sharing and caring, and, in its place, the Medieval Church was found vying with, even exceeding, the State in its aggressive acquisitivenes.

It is indeed a sad story of a dubious Church-State relationship, but, happily, it is not the whole story.

For, side by side with this Erastian development, there was the thin thread of Apostolic Christianity continuing and developing. The early followers of Christ were close to him, and even knew men who had seen and talked with him. They understood, therefore, how he expected them to live, and endeavoured to carry this out. This Apostolic Church continued to meet and worship, without any buildings and with very little popular support, for nearly three hundred years. As described in the Book of the Acts of the Apostles, it contains a blueprint for any genuine future Christian community.

But, when the Church obtained official recognition, it became swamped by the influx of popular nominal Christians, and was unable to survive this mass impact of conforming citizens of the Roman Empire. But the Christian ideal survived. Groups of sincere followers carried it on, and, half a century later, we find strong tributes being paid to this Early Church by some of the Church Fathers, the thinkers, writers, and acknowledged learned Churchmen of the period.

These men were beginning to realise that something had indeed gone wrong with the Church. It had lost its early idealism and enthusiasm. It had compromised with the State. It was now a mere appendage of the secular power, acquiescing in much that was unworthy, and accommodating itself to the prevailing low standards of Society: it had indeed, as one of them pointed out, become 'staid'.

A study of the works of the Church Fathers of the fourth century A.D. is most revealing. For they continually bewail the passing of the Apostolic Church and refer to its activities as the golden age of true Christianity. It is certainly worth considering a few examples of their preaching. The following will give some idea of the attitude they took up:

St. Ambrose, the great bishop of Milan (339–397) says in one of his sermons:—

"It is not yours that you give to the poor, it is his. What was given for the common use of all, do you alone appropriate? The earth is all men's, not the property of the rich."

St. Chrysostom (347–407) famed preacher of Antioch and Constantinople, emphasises the points:—

"It is not for lack of miracles that the Church is staid, it is because we have forsaken the Angelic life of Pentecost, and fallen back on private property. If we lived as they did, with all things common, we should soon convert the whole world, with no need of miracles at all." (HOMILY 25 on ACTS).

St. Cyril, Bishop of Jerusalem in AD.362, writes thus:—

"So great also was the grace of the Holy Spirit, which wrought by means of the twelve Apostles in them who believed, that they were of one heart and one soul, and their enjoyment of their goods was common, the, possessors piously offering the price of their possessions, and no one among them was wanting ought." (HOMILY ON THE ACTS II).

St. Basil, of Caesarea (329–379) gives the following advice:—

"Let us earnestly endeavour ourselves after the first arrangement of the Christians; for they had all things in common, – life, soul, united action, a common table, an unbroken brotherhood, love unfeigned, many bodies working at one task, different souls composed to one consent." (HOMILIA DICTA TEMPORE FAMIS ET SICCITATIS).

And, Pope Gregory (540–604) in his answers to St. Augustine's queries about his missionary work in England, replied simply:—

"You are to follow the course of life which our forefathers did in the time of the Primitive Church, when none of them said anything he possessed was his own, but all things were in common among them". (BEDE. ANGLO-SAXON CHRONICLE).

But it was not the leaders of the Church – the wealthy hierarchy of archbishops, bishops and cardinals – who were listening to what these learned Fathers had to say. The prelates were too busy, involved in political manoeuvring, and national and international intrigue. Living a life of luxury and surrounded by large sycophantic entourages, they were far removed from what was going on at the grass roots. Their episcopal ears were certainly not on the ground, and they knew, and cared, nothing about the people. "Jacques Bonhomme", "Herr Everybody" and even "Walter, the tiler" were unknown to them. They would not even recognise them as human beings at all, if they ever saw them.

It was in the ranks of the mendicant friars and parochial chaplains, the "clerical proletariat", as they have been called, that the message of the Church Fathers was received, taken into their hearts, and bore fruit. A strong Christian radical tradition was growing and developing in Europe and England at this time, and this was carried far and wide by these chaplains. As they preached, it soon became apparent that the Christian belief could be a revolutionary creed in the hands of the common people.

Rodney Hilton, in his study of the Peasants' Revolt, *Bond Men Made Free*,[1] writes of the parish clergy as follows:—

> "The better they knew the Bible and the writings of the Fathers of the Church, the more explosive the mixture of social and religous radicalism was likely to be. Here they had to hand an enormous repository of ideas, some of which could be as profoundly critical of the social order as other ideas, from the same repository, could bolster up that same order."

In England, in the second half of the fourteenth century, this explosive mixture of social and religous radicalism never entered a more receptive and enthusiastic mind and heart than that of a young parochial chaplain in Britain's oldest recorded town of Colchester in Essex. His name was John Ball.

---

[1] Temple Smith, London, 1973, p. 210.

CHAPTER 3

The Origin of John Ball

IN one of his allegorical letters, John Ball, leader of the great Peasants' Revolt of 1381, described himself as "Sometime Saint Mary priest of York and now of Colchester". The ecclesiastical position he held in Colchester was that of parochial chaplain at St. James', East Hill, of which the incumbent was, strangely enough, a priest bearing the same name as himself. Contemporary chronicles refer to John Ball as a chaplain, and, Lindsay and Groves in their *The Peasants' Revolt of 1381*,[1] describe him as a parochial chaplain of St. James whose work centred at Colchester for thirty years. He is mentioned in the Colchester Court Rolls of May 11th 1377 together with a fellow chaplain. And the Calendar of Patent Rolls, 1374–1377, describes him as a chaplain.

Parochial chaplains, in medieval times, occupied a status which, in the Church of today, would be that of assistant curate. They have been described as the clerical proletariat of the Middle Ages.[2] Most of them came from peasant families and, consequently, understood and sympathised with the serfs living under depressing conditions. Thus, they usually made common cause with the workers and took part in their revolts. A modern parallel might be the worker-priests in France who supported the workers' struggles, joined the Communist Party and whose movement was, consequently, banned by the Pope.

In the small guide to St. James's Church, written by a former rector, Canon M. M. Martin, in 1969, John Ball is described as a national character, whose preaching on Christian democracy led to the banding together of the peasants in revolt against an incompetent government.[3]

The *Encyclopedia Brittanica* states that John Ball was an agitator for about twenty years before the uprising began,

---

[1] Hutchinson 1950.
[2] See "The English Church in the 14th Century" by W. A. Pantin, C.U.P. 1955.
[3] He is wrongly described as the rector of St. James.

and that he gained notoriety by inflammatory sermons advocating a classless society. It adds that knowledge of Ball's career is derived almost entirely from prejudiced chroniclers.

The *Dictionary of National Biography* gives the further information that he was probably over forty years of age when he became so conspicuous in history. It states that he was certainly living in Essex in the year 1366/67 when the Dean of Bocking was ordered to cite him to appear before the Archbishop of Canterbury and to forbid persons to attend his preaching (*See Appendix I*). Ten years later there was an order for his arrest, as an excommunicate priest, addressed to some of the clergy in the neighbourhood of Colchester (*See Appendix II*). His first recorded excommunication was, however, in 1364, by Simon of Sudbury, Bishop of London (subsequently Archbishop of Canterbury).[1]

D. W. Coller, the Essex historian, writing over one hundred years ago, states that John Ball went about the country preaching the doctrine of equality in its widest sense, the right of all to the soil, and inveighing against the insolence of one class in setting up distinctions of superiority over another.

Until recently, this was about all that was known about the antecedents of John Ball. His origin and place of birth had never been discovered. But towards the end of 1975, a typescript volume turned up in the reference department of Colchester Public Library. This was a history of the village of Peldon in Essex by a Mrs Kay Gilmour, who had died in 1955, shortly after completing it.

This exhaustive study of this tiny marshland villae some 7 miles from Colchester on the Essex coast, opposite Mersea Island, contained evidence that John Ball, leader of the Peasants' Revolt, was indeed a native of Peldon. This proof was found in the Colchester Court Rolls as follows:—

COLCHESTER COURT ROLLS VOL. I p. 229
(Benham and Jeayes transcript)

HUNDRED. MONDAY AFTER CONVERSION OF ST. PAUL (30th January 1352)

---

[1] See *Registrum S. de Sudbiria* (Canterbury & York Society), Volume II, p. 138.

TENEMENT "FOR LIFE" BETWEEN EAST AND WEST STOCKWELL STREETS

"Joan, widow of Wm. Balle, of Peldon, produced a charter before the bailiffs, which John, son and heir of William, coming of age and being admitted tenant, acknowledged. The charter was as follows: "Grant by John, son and heir of Wm. Balle, of Peldon, to Joan, his mother, of a tenement in Colchester between Eststokwellestr. and Weststokwellestrat for her life.

Witness; Matthew J. Roberte and Robert Fraunceys, Bailiffs, Adam Waryn, Wm. Hadleye, Richard Evesyng, Warin Parker, Robert Beche, clerk. Dated Feast of St. Petronilla, 24th Edward III (31st May 1350)."

COLCHESTER COURT ROLLS VOL. I p. 239

HUNDRED. MONDAY AFTER FEAST OF ST. MAGDALEN (23 July 1352)

"Thomas de la Neylond produced a charter by which Joan, widow of William Balle, granted to him a tenement in St. Martin's Parish, Colchester, in Eststokwellstret. Dated Saturday after Feast of St. James, 26th Edward III (i.e. 28th July 1352).

The same produced a charter, dated same date, by which John, son and heir of Wm. Balle of Peldon, released to him his claim in the same tenement in Eststokwellstret."

Mrs Gilmour makes the following points:—
1) Why would a young man of nineteen give over a house, inherited from his deceased father, to his mother who did not need it, as she promptly disposed of it? The answer is for the simple reason that, as he was about to begin training as a celibate priest, he would not be able to own it. He confirmed this "for life" on coming of age in 1352.
2) Everything in John Ball's letters indicate that he was of rural origin.
3) It is recorded that, for many years before he became a parochial chaplain at St. James's Church, he was in the

neighbourhood of Colchester, to the annoyance of the ecclesiastical authorities. Soon after training at St. Mary's Abbey, York, he come back to what was his home ground.

4) John Ball had a detailed knowledge of, and a very great sympathy with, the plight of the rural peasants. In Peldon, the serfs were particularly oppressed, as the Lord of the Manor at this period was none other than Michael de la Pole, Admiral of England, who participated with the Black Prince in the brutal sack of Limoges in 1370, was one of Richard II's 'evil councillors' and subsequently became Chancellor.

To this perhaps inconclusive evidence of the late Mrs Gilmour, I would add the following:–

1) In spite of orders for his apprehension issued by successive Archbishops, Islip, Langham and Sudbury, John Ball was able to avoid arrest for years, and to roam at will. This leads to the conclusion that he was a local man who knew the terrain intimately, and had friends and relatives in the area who gave him shelter. The village of Peldon is an isolated one, in a marshy coastal district of Essex, often shrouded in mist and sea fog, an ideal hiding place for someone on the run who was familiar with the neighbourhood from early life.

2) After the fall of Colchester to the rebels, early in the revolt, one of the first manors they proceeded to destroy was that of Peldon. In addition to this, they sacked the house of Admiral Edmund de la Mare in the village, a relative of the hated Abbot de la Mare of St. Albans. Bundles of Admiralty papers were stuck on pitchforks and carried before the local Peldon rebels when they marched with the others on London.[1]

3) There was undoubted regular two-way traffic between Colchester and York in medieval times, particularly in ecclesiastical affairs, where the link was strong. As far back as 1096, Stephen, Abbot of St. Mary's Abbey, York, had sent thirteen of his Benedictine monks down to Colchester to establish the newly-built St. John's Abbey there, at the

---

[1] See *The Great Revolt of 1381* by Charles Oman (O.U.P. 1906), p. 47.

request of its founder, Eudo Dapifer, steward of William the Conqueror, and town overlord. Many young Colchester aspirants to the priesthood would, in all probability, be directed to York for their training.

4) From the proceedings mentioned in the Colchester Court Rolls, it is evident that John Ball had attained the age of twenty-one in 1352. This would give his birth date as some time in 1331, and his age, at his execution, as fifty. This is the age which many historians have, hitherto, conjectured to be his age at the time of his death.

This typescript of the late Mrs Gilmour has led to one of the most exciting of historical discoveries in recent times. For we now know the age and origin of one of England's medieval heroes, concerning which historians have been compelled to leave a blank in the books they have written. And we also know the solution to the previous puzzling evidence of John Ball's reappearance in Colchester so soon after becoming a priest, and making it his headquarters for more than a quarter of a century.

CHAPTER 4

John Ball's Views and Relationships

JOHN BALL was a man of wide vision and intense sympathy. He witnessed the plight of the English people, kept in servitude by an incompetent and degenerate nobility, and he preached solidly against the social injustices prevailing at the time. And these were found in both the Church and the State.

John Ball's opposition to the Church was not on doctrinal grounds, for he was, by nature, a religious man. He attacked the Church because, owning one-third of the land and a major economic power, it was just as corrupt as the secular nobility. What he preached was nothing more or less than the social implications of Christianity. He was a prophet in the ancient Hebrew style, denouncing the wickedness of the times, and especially that of the higher clergy. He wished to see a Christian democracy established with all social inequalities redressed.

He took, as his sole text, the popular jingle of the period, "When Adam delved and Eve span, who was then the gentleman?".

All this inevitably brought upon him the wrath of both the civil and ecclesiastical authorities. In the course of his ministry, he was, from time to time, imprisoned by successive Archbishops of Canterbury, and finally excommunicated and forbidden to preach.

But he fought back, preaching in churchyards to the people coming out of church whenever he could. In the spring of 1381, Archbishop Simon of Sudbury complained bitterly that Ball had slunk back again into his Diocese, and was still preaching his perfidious doctrines. In April of that year, he was arrested and confined in the Archbishop's prison at Maidstone.

It is obvious that John Ball's ministry at St. James, Colchester, was a somewhat chequered one. But he knew that he had a work to do which took him further than the narrow confines of the parish. He had read the message of the times and did not hesitate to answer the call when it came.

For his championship of the people, and his criticism of the Church, he earned the opprobrium of all the monastic chroniclers of the day. Froissart describes him as "a foolish priest in the county of Kent", (for he was in the Maidstone gaol when the Revolt broke out, and took charge of the rebels when released by them). The *Anonimalle Chronicle* sums up Ball's sermons as "these and many other ravings", and Henry Knighton, Canon of St. Mary's Abbey, Leicester, in the Chronicle that bears his name, mentions that Ball "disturbed many with his own doctrines".

All chroniclers, of this period in English history, monastic or lay, are agreed in seeing John Ball as the 'éminence grise' of the Peasants' Revolt.

Some difficulty has been caused by the strange coincidence that the rector of St. James's Church, Colchester, was also called John Ball. But a study of the Court Rolls of the town has clearly revealed the distinction between the two men.

John Ball, rector of St. James's Church, Colchester, was appointed on March 11th, 1372(3).[1] This is confirmed by the church register, by Newcourt in his *Repertorium Ecclesiasticum,* and by Gurney Benham in a note in the transcription of the Colchester Court Rolls. These all agree that he served as rector until he died in January, 1394. There are several references in the Rolls to this John, Rector of St. James, before the Revolt, and one, **after** it, in 1383, which reads,

> "*HUNDRED. MONDAY AFTER FEAST OF ST. AMBROSE (April 6th, 1383)*
> John (Ball), rector of St. James, fine for trespass, by pledge of James Goldsmyth" (Vol. IV, p. 163).

The John Ball, chaplain, appears in the Rolls as follows:—

---

[1] See Le Neve's *Fasti Ecclesiae Anglicanae,* and Archbishop Sudbury's *Registrum.*

"I, UNDRED. AFTER FEAST OF ST. DUNSTAN (May 11th 1377)
Wm. Crabbe, in reply to John Balle and John Proude, chaplains, who say that Wm. Crabbe entered their house in Est Strat without licence or warrant and, by force took certain goods and vessels away, says that he took the same for rent due to him and unpaid; Complainants say he had no "status" in said house. Day given" (Vol. III, p. 139).

"HUNDRED. FEAST OF ST. LAURENCE (AUG. 9th) I RICH. II (1377)
Andrew Danel and John Danel, accused of assaulting John, clerk of St. James, plead that they acted in self-defence. Enquiry ordered" (Vol. III, p. 152).

Thus, there were two John Balls at St. James – one the incumbent and the other the parochial chaplain. This may be a mere coincidence, but it is more than likely that they were actually related. John Ball, the Revolt leader, was in such disfavour with the Church authorities that no one but a relative would be likely to offer him any employment. So we can assume that John Ball, rector of St. James could have been an uncle or cousin, who, for reasons of family ties, gave this wild young priest a job.

And, as the Rolls clearly indicate, the two priests, rector and parochial chaplain, lived in different residences, the former in the rectory, and the latter in the house in East Street which he shared with his fellow chaplain as tenants. Also, the incumbent is always referred to as "John, rector of St. James", whereas John Ball is designated as "chaplain" or merely "clerk".

Researchers in the past have been confused over these two John Balls, and their true relationship can now be made known. When the printed but unpublished pages of Volume IV of the Colchester Court Rolls transcribed by Gurney Benham just before he died in 1944 and which had been kept in the muniments room of Colchester Castle, became available for study in May 1976, it was possible to find the clues herein mentioned. And Benham, himself, supports these in a note he made in Volume III to the effect that this JOHN BALLE, who was involved with his fellow chaplain in a dispute with their landlord, might conceivably be the famous priest who took a leading part in Wat Tyler's insurrection in 1381 (VOL. III, p. 139).

In the last volume he edited (VOL. IV), Benham adds the following sad note:

> ROLLS FOR THE YEAR, 1380–1381, WHEN ALEXIUS COGGERE AND RALPH ALGAR WERE BAILIFFS, ARE MISSING. This is to be regretted as this year is marked in the OATH BOOK as "ANNO RUMORIS" (the year of Disturbance). It was memorable for the rising in which Wat Tyler, Jack Straw and John Ball (St. Mary Priest, of Colchester) were leaders".

It is indeed to be regretted that the Court Rolls of Colchester for the vital year of September 1380 to September 1381 are missing, as the late Mr Benham sadly notes. Some of these were obviously destroyed during the Rising, as will be revealed in a later chapter, and the Reverend Philip Morant, Colchester rector and historian, who produced his celebrated history of the town in 1748, undoubtedly had access to these Rolls, but also possessed the unfortunate habit of using only those he thought important and throwing the rest away!

But the priest referred to as "St. Mary Priest of Colchester" is well recorded as the leader of the 1381 Peasants' Revolt in most standard history books, though many of these are somewhat inaccurate with regard to his place of origin, slavishly following the incorrect statement of chronicler Froissart, who himself was neither an Englishman nor an actual eye-witness of the Revolt.

American historian George Kriehn's article on the English Peasants' Revolt of 1381 in the *American Historical Review* of 1901–1902, contains what is perhaps the most detailed and scholarly account of part of the Rising which has been written. In this he states categorically that both John Ball and his fellow leader, Wat Tyler, came from Colchester where, he affirms the Revolt was originally planned and organised. Having established beyond doubt the identity of Wat Tyler, he adds:—

> "It is interesting to know, as well as confirmatory of the above conclusion, that John Ball, prophet and chief

organiser of the Revolt, was likewise of Colchester, from which, as I hope to show at some future time, the Revolt was originally fostered and organised".[1]

The latest assessment of John Ball is to be found in a Thesis submitted to the Virginia State University in America in November 1976, for her Master's Degree in History, by Sandra Jane Eccli, entitled *English Criticism of Ecclesiastical Institutions in the 1370's*. Mrs Eccli states:–

"During the 1360's and 1370's, Ball regarded Colchester as his home. It was a good town for a libertarian. The medieval borough government was 'singularly democratic', and, of all the English towns, Colchester has the longest history of social and religious radicalism. The fourteenth-century Colchester Court Rolls have been printed to the year 1379,[2] as have the borough records for the entire medieval period. They reveal a swarming social life full of personal altercations, business disputes, political squabbles, women's liberation struggles and continual battles with the town's two largest monasteries, St. John's Abbey and St. Botolph's Priory.

"The town had its share of troublemaker clerics in the 1370's. Chaplain John Fuller liked to wrestle for a wager but would fail to pay if he lost. And there was John Isenmongre, another chaplain, who was continually hauled before the magistrates, for poaching, trespass and even assault. It is gratifying to look through the records and find that, although the name of 'John Ball' or 'Balle' is mentioned many times, he was not that sort of man. In July, 1363, the Prior of St. Botolph's Priory, leading a gang of toughs, assaulted a monk of St. John's Abbey. The names of the gang members were given in the records. Ball's was not among them, of course, but the incident may have inspired him to preach bitter sermons denouncing monasticism, which could have led to the troubled situation he was facing in February, 1364."

I am glad to have the opportunity of including this tribute

---

[1] *Studies in the Sources of the Social Revolt of 1381*, p. 459.
[2] Now discovered to 1383.

to John Ball from my friend, Sandra Eccli, of Arlington, Virginia,[1] one of the most indefatigable of researchers at present working in this field.

---

[1] Now resident in Utica, Michigan.

CHAPTER 5

Fourteenth Century Conditions in England

TO understand why this Colchester clergyman became a national leader, it is necessary to examine the conditions under which the people of England were living at this period.

The Black Death, of 1348–49, had wiped out approximately one third of the population of the country. This resulted in a shortage of labour, and a consequent demand by the peasants for better conditions. The response of the Government was to bring in the Statute of Labourers in 1351, in an attempt to force the people to remain in the conditions of serfdom which existed before the onset of the plague.

It must be remembered that the working people at this time were living in a state of near-slavery. They possessed few rights, and were treated by lords and nobility not much better than animals, to be disposed of like chattels.

No girl could get married without the consent of the lord of the manor. When she married, a fine of 'merchet' was exacted from her father, and if she had a child out of wedlock, a further fine of 'leyrewite' was demanded. On the death of a tenant, a fine of 'heriot' was due before his heir could inherit any of his meagre possessions, and, on top of all this, a 'mortuary' fine, in which the lord took from the deceased his best beast, his best suit of clothes, and his best tools. In the case of a woman, it was her best dress and best bed that was demanded! And to cap it all – under the 'mortuary' fine, the Church, which, at that time, owned one-third of the land in England, took the second best of everything, in addition to tithes during lifetime!

The serfs were obliged to perform three days unpaid work per week on the manors of their lords, before they could look after their own little holdings. This was known as 'week work' and, in addition, they had to provide 'boon work' at busy times like hay time and harvest, irrespective of the condition of their own crops. Their lords always had priority of claim in the matter of their time and labour.

The condition of the working people in this century was aptly described in a monkish lampoon of the period which stated, "What could a serf do but serve? A pure serf he shall be, lacking liberty, and his son after him".

Deeds of sale at that time simply stated, "Know that I have sold .... nativum meum (my villein), and all his offspring, born or to be born".

Little wonder that the Abbot of Burton, writing about the position of the ordinary folk in the fourteenth century, should have stated that the villeins owned "nihil praeter ventrum", nothing but their bellies!

In addition, further burdens were being placed on the peasantry. This was through a succession of Poll Taxes. The need for these taxes was to pay for a number of disastrous foreign military expeditions. The Hundred Years' War had been raging, on and off, since 1337. And these intermittant expeditions to France, and battles fought there, were a constant drain on the national economy. The King, Richard II, and his advisers had to find the money somewhere. And Poll Taxes were the answer.

Three Poll Taxes were imposed in quick succession. The first, in 1377, was a tax of one groat, (4d) per head on all from the age of 14 years and upwards. This was followed, in 1379, by a graduated tax in which the tax was varied according to status, the nobility paying more than the workers. This was the fairest of all the taxes, but it was not liked by the nobles and often evaded. Consequently, a third tax, of three groats per head, from 15 years and upwards, was introduced in 1380. This bore heavily on the peasants and town workers and was one of the main causes of the revolt.

Thus, the common people, becoming conscious of a growing feeling that they had a destiny, were more and more restive. They were prepared to demand an end to serfdom, an end to week and boon work. They wanted freedom from crippling taxes, freedom to buy and sell, the right to be taken on as free tenants of their land at a fair rent of a groat per acre, and to receive money payments for work done for their lords.

It was into this sort of turbulent atmosphere, with the people restive and frustrated, that John Ball was thrown, coming as a young priest from St. Mary's Abbey in York to the ancient town of Colchester. As a contemporary writer put it, "The people are in such a plight that they can give no more. I suspect that, if they had a leader, they would revolt".

This very highly emotive situation was, of course, not something that was indigenous to England. The same sort of thing was happening, as we have seen, throughout Europe. And, in the fourteenth century, England was very close to Europe indeed, almost an integral part in fact. There were close ties of commerce and trade, a well-knit religious connection of the Church, and kings and nobles of all the countries who had contrived to be related to one another in some way or other. And, with only the short twenty-one miles of the Dover Straits to overcome, travel between England and the Continent became a commonplace. It was certainly very much easier to travel from London to Paris, in those days, than to undertake the hazardous journey from London to York, or Edinburgh.

England's contact with Europe in the fourteenth century was, amazing as it may seem, closer than that which exists at the moment in these days of the European Economic Community!

Historians have said that there was no heretical thinking in England before Wycliffe's Lollardy got really under way in the early fifteenth century. Certainly the first really severe official action against heretics came with the promulgation of the statute *De Heretico Comburendo*, in 1401. So, in the absence of evidence of radical heretical views having developed in England at this period, it is from the wider critical and heretical thinking of Europe, previously mentioned in Chapter 1, that we must look for the stimulus which gave impetus to the Peasants' Revolt.

True, there had been much social criticism in various parts of the country by both orthodox and unorthodox English preachers, but ideas with subversive political implications were common in France, Italy, Germany, and elsewhere at the time, and these were now coming in to England. Stemming from the great communistic traditions of the Church Fathers, these ideas undoubtedly influenced peasant leaders such as Jack Straw, Wat Tyler and John Ball.

And, significantly, ordinary folk of England were now developing a completely novel idea of their own. This was that government by the commons was now possible, and even necessary, for the country. When the Revolt developed, the people fought under the slogan, 'With King Richard and the *True Commons*'! They realised, for the first time, that although they were not represented in parliament, and had no voice in government, they could be the ruling power. No longer was this hierarchy of nobles and ministers, with their self-assumed, God-given superiority, inviolable. These were proving now that they had feet of clay and could be toppled over.

What gave the common people of England this new-found assurance in the fourteenth century was the fact that so many of them had served as archers in the French Wars, and, from the time of the battle of Crecy in 1346, onwards, had begun to realise their superiority. This great battle indicated, for the first time, the fact that common foot soldiers proved themselves more than a match for heavily armed knights; it marked the first sign of the decay of feudalism. Standing together, shoulder to shoulder, with their homemade weapons, constructed from village churchyard yews, the peasants were able to defeat these seemingly god-like men in shining armour, mounted on huge destriers and wielding deadly maces or long swords. In the bloodbath of Crecy and other battles of the period, the flower of the French nobility had indeed indicated their Achilles heels. In three great victories, in which they had been the decisive factors, the commons of England came to realise that they were competent to be the rulers of their own country in the future.

It was thus that there began to develop in England at this time, an organisation of the people, binding them together in a determination to achieve their liberty and ultimately to rule their country. This came to be known as "Magna Societas" – "The Great Society". It was variously referred to as "The Great Company", "The Great Fellowship", or simply "The Commune".

CHAPTER 6

What Was "The Great Society"?

FOR many years now, historians have been divided in their opinions about the existence of this "Great Society". Some researchers can find evidence only of what were called "confederacies and conspiracies" among the workers. Thus, Charles Oman refers to the villeins in 1377 "confederating themselves into 'conventicles' to resist their lord's service".[1]

Edgar Powell, however, in his much quoted work, *The Rising in East Anglia in 1381*,[2] writes about the Revolt as follows:

"It was the matured result of a comprehensive plan, carried out by means of a more or less perfect organisation, extending throughout the Eastern Counties."

This, he adds, extended as far north as the Humber.

G. M. Trevelyan, author of *England in the Age of Wycliffe*,[3] supports this view when he writes that the English Rising was stimulated by messengers from Essex asking for support "in accordance with the plan of co-operation framed by the Great Society". He states also that "agitators now came bearing not general exhortations but a particular command from the Great Society as they called the union of the lower classes which they were attempting to form". Referring the situation in Kent, he adds that "word was sent to the disturbed districts that no one, on pain of death, was to do custom or service to his lord without orders from the Great Society".

Rodney Hilton considers that these "particular commands"

---

[1] Op.cit., p. 10.
[2] Cambridge University Press, 1896, p. 57.
[3] Longman, 1899, pp. 209, 203, 219.

27

were nothing more than cryptic letters, loaded with allegorical and symbolic meanings. Some of these, recorded by chroniclers Walsingham and Knighton, are, he maintains, attributable to John Ball, and contain recognisable echoes from Langland's *Vision of Piers Plowman*. He suggests that the Latin "Magna Societas" could equally well be translated as "the large company", "the great band", or "the big gang".[1]

Lindsay and Groves, state definitely that the Revolt was planned, prepared and organised by a widespread organisation called the Great Society or Great Fellowship. It had agents working for years in the towns and villages, and the genius who created it was none other than John Ball. The authors add that events overwhelmingly support the argument for such an organisation.[2]

R. H. Hilton and H. Fagan, in their book *The English Rising of 1381*,[3] are not quite so definitive. They admit that there was some organisation or ideological preparation for the Revolt, but no "Great Society". They suggest that there was some common understanding between village and village, and region and region.

But, R. B. Dobson, in his study in depth, *The Peasants' Revolt of 1381*,[4] can find no evidence of any vast conspiratorial organisation underlying the Revolt, and affirms that there is slender evidence of any peasant underground movement. But he does record the reference to "Magna Societas" in the trial records of East Anglia and Kent.

However, there is ample evidence that such a society did exist. There are references, in the contemporary chronicles, to men who rode around the countryside with messages from the Great Society, and their names are given. Most historians have made mention of these.

There was Adam Clymme, or Ely, who was subsequently hanged there, who urged people to join the movement and to cease performing any service of custom due to their lords, "except as he might inform them on behalf of the Great

---

[1] Op.cit., pp. 214/15.
[2] Op.cit.
[3] Lawrence & Wishart, 1950.
[4] Macmillan, 1970.

Society". Both Powell and Lindsay and Groves refer to this statement.

Then there was a certain George de Dunsby, from Lincolnshire, referred to by Dobson (quoting from chronicler Henry Knighton), who, when charged with inciting men to rise, said "he was a messenger of the Great Society and had been sent to the town of St. Edmunds to make the commons of that town rise". With him was another messenger, John Wright, and the rising in the Lincoln village of Dunsby, led by the parish priest, William Swepston, was one of the few recorded risings in that county.

Thomas Sweyne, of Coggeshall in Essex, is also mentioned as a trusty messenger of the Great Society, as is John Shirle, of Cambridge, who was tactless enough to say in a tavern in that city, on July 16th 1381, that "the King's ministers deserved hanging rather than John Ball who was an honest man", and was himself promptly hanged for his own honesty of expression.

At the trials of these and many other messengers of the Great Society after the collapse of the Revolt, they all protested their innocence and insisted that they were merely serving the community. As Charles Oman reports, these men went to their death maintaining that they had served the commons faithfully. He adds that there were no detailed records preserved of the their trial which, if there had been, might have shown that they were conscientious and manly supporters who joined the Rising not for plunder, but to win freedom, and serve some even more ideal end.[1]

Thus, it would appear that there certainly is support for the view that the "Magna Societas" did exist in England from the mid-fourteenth century onwards as historians and chroniclers have confirmed. Hilton and Fagan, in their work previously quoted, state that, as soon as the rebels were granted their charters by King Richard II, at the Mile End meeting on June 14th, messenges from the Great Society were sent immediately into Norfolk, Suffolk, Cambridgeshire and Huntingdonshire to report this.

And the defence of men on trial, after the collapse of the

---

[1] Op.cit., p. 136.

Revolt, was unshakenly the claim that they were acting as agents of the Great Society.

Perhaps the most convincing piece of evidence that such an organisation as this did exist, lies in the fact that the Revolt spread so spontaneously and rapidly throughout the countryside. This could only have happened as a result of careful planning.

CHAPTER 7

Influences on John Ball

JOHN BALL was not Froissart's "foolish priest", nor was he "a chaplain of evil disposition" as stated by the author of the *Anonimalle Chronicle*. Rather was he a representative of the strong Christian radical tradition, prevalent in both England and Europe at this time.

In England there was emerging a body of clergy who, reacting against the luxury and corruption of the Church, were now opposing it and preaching boldly the practical application of primitive Christianity. These men, drawn from the ranks of the mendicant friars, might well be described as the earliest Lollards, the proto-Lollards, who were communistic in outlook. And their influence was a strong one on anyone who might be thinking that there was something wrong with the society of the day. And there were those, in the town of Colchester and its surroundings, who were thinking just this.

One such was this priest, John Ball, parochial chaplain at one of the town's churches. A profound thinker, he possessed considerable political judgment. His name is in every English history book, but few give a correct assessment of his character, of the real part he played in the Revolt, and of what he actually stood for.

The evidence about John Ball is derived almost entirely from the contemporary chroniclers, Froissart, Walsingham, Knighton, and the author of the *Anonimalle Chronicle*. These, with the exception of Froissart, were monks, naturally antagonistic to Ball, owing to his criticism of the Church, and provide, therefore, a very biased view of his life and work. And Froissart himself was not an eye-witness but relied on hearsay.

But what has confused the issue very much is the view held

by these contemporary writers that John Ball was a follower of John Wycliffe, the reputed Lollard leader, a view which many historians have persisted in maintaining up to the present age. This is often supported by quoting a spurious confession of Ball's before he was hanged in 1381, that, for two years previously, he had been a disciple of Wycliffe. But this is now a completely discredited report.

The facts are that John Ball was preaching his revolutionary doctrines for more than 20 years before Wycliffe emerged on the scene. The teaching of the two men is totally different – Wycliffe was a reformer, John Ball was a revolutionary. Wycliffe, always a firm supporter of the Establishment, was hostile to the Revolt. He never incited men to revolution, and deprecated the actual Rising itself. None of the numerous priests who took part in it were known to be followers of Wycliffe, and there is no evidence that the insurgents showed any signs of Wycliffite tendencies.

Historian, Margaret Aston, writing in the journal *Past and Present* in April 1960, under the heading "Lollardy and Sedition 1381–1431" states:–

"There are no grounds to believe in John Ball's alleged association with Wycliffe, and considerable research has yielded no evidence to support the view that Wycliffe's teaching, or Lollard preaching, were either significant instruments, or in any way connected with the 1381 Revolt".

But the idea has still persisted that there was a connection between Lollardy and the Revolt, and this could be maintained only if it were realised that John Wycliffe did not represent the whole spectrum of Lollardy. The identification of Lollardy solely with John Wycliffe has led to much confusion of thought.

There was, however, a considerable body of opinion at the time of the Revolt, which accused all Lollards of being behind it. There were certain aspects of Wycliffe's teaching which supported this view. The Lollards' desire to abolish the temporalities of the Church led to a demand for the abolition of all temporalities, sacred or secular.

So, criticism of the Church tended to become criticism of society as a whole, and what started as a religous heresy could soon develop into an attack on the established order. But

Wycliffe never intended to attack the feudal system but, in attacking the international Church, he weakened one of the greatest bulwards of that system, and, indirectly, may be said to have contributed to its destruction.

Thus, the view is still held, in some circles today, that Wycliffe and his Lollards were, somehow, behind the Peasant's Revolt, in spite of the evidence given that there was little sign of social revolution in the aims of most of his followers, and that much opposition to tithe payments was by no means exclusively Lollard, but had its origin in the teaching of the mendicant orders.[1]

These mendicant friars, preaching a definite communistic political doctrine, which they inherited from the Church Fathers, were the real radical Lollards. They were openly accused by the monastic writers of the time of being responsible for the rebellion, and they were the most bitter enemies of Wycliffe. (His "Poor Preachers" had nothing to do with the Revolt, for their period of activity actually came just after it).

The friars were the only clergy favoured by the rebels, who according to Jack Straw's confession, were to be allowed to continue if the Revolt had succeeded. Langland in his *Piers Plowman*, accuses them of preaching philosophic communism in the words:–

"They preach men of Plato, and prove it by Seneca

That all things under heaven ought to be in common."

John Ball, himself, found a considerable measure of accord with the friars who undoubtedly influenced him. In his preaching, he emphasised that, in order to establish a just and fair society, it was necessary to remove the hierarchy of both Church and State. In enumerating the corrupt leaders who would have to go, archbishops, bishops, higher clergy, etc. – he, rather significantly, exempted the friars. The following are extracts from the *Anonimalle Chronicle*, written by a monk of St. Mary's Abbey, York, indicating John Ball's exemption of friars from condemnation (transcribed by G. M. Trevelyan, translated by Charles Oman).

"At this time, the commons had as their councillor a

---

[1] See *The Later Lollards*, by John A. F. Thompson (O.U.P. 1965), p. 247.

chaplain of evil disposition named Sir John Ball, which Sir John advised them to get rid of all the lords, and of the archbishop and bishops, and abbots and priors, and most of the monks and canons, saying that there should be no bishop in England save one archbishop only, and that he himself would be that prelate, and they would have no monks or canons in religious houses save two, and that their possessions should be distributed among the laiety. For which sayings he was esteemed among the commons as a prophet, and laboured with them day by day to strengthen them in their malice, – and a fit reward he got, when he was hung, drawn, and quartered, and beheaded as a traitor . . .''

". . . And the said knight came to the King telling him that he had heard from hs servant, who had been in the hands of the rebels that day, . . . and that their purpose was to slay all the lords and ladies of great renown, and all the archbishops, bishops, abbots and priors, monks and canons, parsons and vicars, by the advice of the aforesaid Sir John Ball.''

Historian May McKisack, in the *Oxford History of England – 14th Century, 1307–1399,* writes:–

"Even if all the prelates are to be slain, John Ball will be there to assume their functions; if the rich possessioners are removed, the mendicants will suffice for the administration of the sacraments''.

Possibly John Ball had got to know some of the Franciscans while a parochial chaplain at St. James, Colchester, for, just across the road from this Church, lay the great monastery of the Grey Friars, founded in the early 14th Century by Lord Fitzwalter of Lexden.

The friars' political philosophy was certainly not the sort of thing to which Wycliffe would have given his support. Such views would have been anathema to him. For he was merely a reformer to whom history has erroneously given the leadership of the true Lollard movement, a revolutionary cause wishing to change the society of the day. Wycliffe was no leader of the real Lollards. It is truer to say that John Ball was. Wycliff's type of

Lollardy was primarily a theological movement. True Lollardy was not concerned with niceties of ecclesiastical doctrine. It sought to bring about a new political and economic way of life based on Christian rather than on Church principles.

The sudden outburst of Lollardy in the years following the Peasants' Revolt would indicate that such a development came from something more than the theological writings of an Oxford scholar. There was a force behind this new Lollard revolt which was similar in strength and origin to that which was behind the recent revolt of the peasants. In fact, the Lollard risings of 1414, and of 1431, were very much like 1381 all over again.

There is much evidence to prove this. At the trial of the Lollard heretic, Ralph Mungyn, in Kent, in 1428, he said that "all goods should be held in common, and that no one ought to be allowed to have property.".

Hoccleve, writing in 1415, stated that "community of property was the Lollards' slogan".

Meikeljohn in his *History of England and Great Britain* states that "there was a strong political element in Lollardism" and that "the germ of socialism no doubt existed in the Lollard doctrine".

And we have further evidence that the Lollard mendicant friars had been preaching the communism of the Church Fathers when a certain Thomas Bagley, vicar of Manudon in Essex, was burnt at Smithfield in 1431. In a vain attempt to save his life, he recanted by saying that he now wished to adhere to the views of Wycliffe, rather than those of Jerome, Augustine, Gregory and Ambrose, previously held.[1]

Many more historians now accept this "mendicant friar–Lollard" connection, and agree that some form of Lollardy was indeed behind the Revolt. Therefore, in order to get a clear picture, we must discard Wycliffe entirely as having any major influence on the basic Lollard tradition which was behind the Rising. Rodney Hilton, of Birmingham University, one of the leading authorities on this period, writes:–

"Perhaps the now discarded idea of a close link between

---

[1] See *The Later Lollards*, by John A. F. Thompson, p. 122.

Lollardy and the Rising of 1381 was not, after all, so mistaken, provided that we regard Lollardy as something wider simply than the following of Wycliffe".[1]

Hilton goes on to say that it would not be unreasonable to regard John Ball as a sort of proto-Lollard. In view of this, therefore, any enquiry concerning Lollardy and revolt in the Colchester area is a relevant one. For the restless chaplain at St. James's Church in that town was one of its first real Lollards, drawing together all those who, like himself, had absorbed the revolutionary teaching of the mendicant friars, themselves already known as Lollards.

Hilton adds:–

"However John Ball was clearly not a man like Sloth. His reported sayings are in the long tradition of Christian social radicalism which goes back to St. Ambrose of Milan, if not before".[2]

It is, therefore, to the assistant priest of St. James's Church, Colchester, that credit must be given in connection with the Lollardy and revolt of the latter part of the fourteenth century. His Lollardy was that of the friars, ever active and prominent in the town, and it spread to many others in the district who became associated with him in the famous Revolt that was planned within the walls of Britain's oldest recorded town.

---

[1] Op. cit., p. 213.
[2] Op. cit., p. 211. (See "The Communism of St. Ambrose", in *Essays in the History of Ideas*, by A. C. Lovejoy, 1948)

CHAPTER 8

John Ball's Letters

THE famous letters of John Ball, sent to the Essex peasants and distributed far and wide, were, of necessity, written in a kind of cipher. In one of them, his own identity is masked under the name of 'Shepherd', but his former office at St. Mary's Abbey, York, and his present associations at Colchester, are clearly mentioned. The names of some of the recipients are likewise disguised. John Nameless, John Miller, and John Carter are obvious examples. And there is revealed a strong peasant fear of the townsmen, in the ominous words, "Beware of treachery in the city".

In this letter, Ball was certainly a prophet of the doom that was to come in London. But, in spite of this, the letters do indicate an almost childlike belief that God must inevitably be on the side of the ragged battalions.

The exact date of these compositions is not known. Historians are not agreed about this. Oman is of the opinion that they were written after John Ball's release from prison, Hilton considers that they could have been penned at any time during the course of the Rising, and Dobson states that they were possibly circulating quite widely throughout England during the year 1381.

These letters do make a valuable contribution to the literature of protest in the second half of the fourteenth century. This has been clearly emphasised by Basil Cottle in *The Triumph of English 1350–1400.*[1]

Two points in the letters are worth noting. The first is the influence of the writings of the Franciscans. Echoes of these are discernable at times. In English tags copied into the *Fasciculus*

---

[1] Blandford Press, London 1969.

Morum, a medieval Latin prose work, attributed to the friar, Robert Silke, and published about 1350, there are phrases such as "friend and foe", "well and woe" and "might and right" which occur also in Ball's letters and which may be said to indicate that he knew of this Franciscan work, and, perhaps, instinctively, used expressions from it.

The second point to note is the suggestion of millenarian hopes in the letters. Ball uses the expression "Now is the time" in four out of six of them. In this he may be expressing the conviction that the Golden Age of a Society without distinctions of status or wealth may indeed be achieved in the immediate future. It is for this, as he says to the people, that "he has rung your bell!" Millenarian hopes and aspirations were not altogether lacking in England in 1381, and lower clergy like Ball played a large part in proclaiming that the path lay wide open to an egalitarian, even a communistic, millennium.

The six letters attributed to John Ball provide the exception to the fact that the revolutionary peasants of 1381 are only seen through the hostile eyes of their opponents. This small collection of rhyming epistles drew upon folk allegory. They owe their preservation to the chance that the monks, Walsingham and Knighton, decided to insert copies in their narratives of the great Revolt.

These letters not only call for an armed rising of the people but reveal the mind of a mature political thinker. They were inter-related and, obviously, the work of one writer who, in some of them, used pseudonyms. The names of the recipients are 'masonic' rather than genuine names of identifiable rebels.

R. B. Dobson writes of these letters:–

"More generally, the correspondence reveals two essential characteristics of the author and his audience – a strong sense of personal identification with the ideal of a social brotherhood, and a deeply personal devotion to the most simple and literal truths of the Christian relition".[1]

A study of Ball's letters certainly shows that he received a marked influence from William Langland, whose *Vision of Piers Plowman,* one of the finest allegorical poems in the English

---

[1] Op. cit., p. 380.

tongue, was written a few years before the Revolt broke out.

As Professor Skeat suggested long ago, Langland's *Piers Plowman* provides the key to both the precise meaning and cultural milieu of Ball's correspondence.

These letters were readily understood by the ordinary folk. For Langland's poem, published in 1377, had been known for several years, and Ball's letters, couched in a similar allegorical manner, were accepted as a kind of sequel to Langland's work. Langland wrote of the England of the good King and the commune, in which each man had his place, part and station, and all work and life was in the service of God. John Ball built upon this, extended it, and showed how it could indeed be made to come to pass.

The following is a translation of the letters of John Ball:

1) John Ball, *Saint Mary's Priest,* greets well all manner of men and bids them in the name of the Trinity, Father, Son and Holy Spirit, stand manly together in truth. Help truth and truth shall help you.

> Now reigns pride in every place,
> And greed not shy to show its face,
> And lechery with never shame,
> And gluttony with never blame,
> Envy reigns with treason
> And sloth is ever in season.

God help us for now is the time. Amen.

2) John Shepherd, former Saint Mary's priest of York, now of Colchester, greets well John Nameless and John Miller and John Carter, and bids them to beware of treachery in the city. Stand together in God's name, bid Piers Plowman tend to his work, and chastize well Hob the Robber. Take with you John Trueman and all his companions, and no more. And look to one leader and no more.

> John the Miller's ground small, small, small,
> The King's son of heaven shall pay for all.
> Be aware or be at fault,
> Know your friend from your foe;

Take enough and then say "halt!"
Do well and better, flee from sin,
Seek the peace and stay therein.
So bids John Trueman and all his companions.

3) *Jack Miller* asks your help to keep his mill turning right. He
has ground very small; the King's son of heaven shall pay for
all. Make sure your mill goes right, with all four sails, and the
post standing in steadfastness.
   With right and with might, with skill and with will,
   Let might help right and skill go before will,
   And right before might . . . then watch our mill sail!
   But with might before right, and will before skill,
      Then our mill shall fail.

4) Jack Carter prays to you all that you make a good end to
what you have begun.
Do well and ever better and better.
Only in the evening can men praise the day. If the end be
well, then all is well. Let Piers Plowman my brother dwell at
home and prepare our food. I will go with you and help to
prepare your meat and drink, so that none of you fail. See
that Hob the Robber be well chastized for losing your good
opinion. You have great need to take God with you in all your
deeds. For now is the time to be cautious.

5) Jack Trueman tells you to understand that falseness and
guile have reigned too long:
   Truth's been set under lock,
   And falseness reigns in every flock.
No one may come to the truth unless he sings "Sid dedero".
"Speak, spend, and succeed", said John of Bath, and
therefore sin fares as a wild flood, true love (that once was so
good) is away. Now the clergy for wealth work themselves
woe. God give us redress, for now is the time!

6) John Ball greets you all and tells you to understand that he has rung your bell. Now let there be right and might, will and skill. God motivate every idler! Now is the time. Lady, send to Jesu your son, and your son to his father, to make a good end. In the name of the Trinity of what is begun! amen, amen, for love, amen!

In view of the influence of William Langland on John Ball, it will be interesting to compare the work of the two men. The following are some verses from Langland's *Vision of Piers Plowman* taken from the translation of Henry W. Wells in 1935.[1]

"For we are all Christ's creatures, and by his coffer are we wealthy,
And brothers of one blood, beggars and nobles.
Christ's blood on Calvary is the spring of Christendom,
And we became blood brethren there, recovered by one body,
And gentle without exception,
None base or a beggar, but when sin cause it."

"Therefore love we as lief brothers, each laughing with the other,
And each give what he can spare as his goods are needed.
Let each man help the other, for we shall all go hence.
Let us be neither unkind with our goods nor with our cunning and learning,
For no man knows how near he is to be taken from them."

"Therefore I warn you rich, have ruth on poor folk;
Though you are mighty in the moot hall, be meek in your judgements;
For the measure that you mete shall be meted to you;
Your weighs shall weight you when the hour is ready."

"Love is leach of life, and our Lord is with him.
It is the wicket gate that goes to Heaven.

---

[1] Sheed and Ward.

I say now as I said first, with these texts to witness,
When all treasures are tried, Truth is the fairest.
'Love it!' said the lady, 'I may not linger
With my lesson of love', and she left me gently."

" 'Counsel me, Nature' quoth I, 'what craft is best to study?'
'Learn to love', said Nature, 'and leave all others',
'How shall I come by goods to clothe and feed me?'
'If you love me loyally', he said, 'You will lack never
For meat or worldly wearing while life is with you!' "

In the work of both Langland and Ball, a similarity of feeling and expression can be seen. There is a definite indication of humility, coupled with exhortations that "might does not make right". In spite of the strong tone of moral indignation, there are constant references to the need to love one's enemies. Above all, the two men meet in their allegiance to love as the guiding principle in life. Ball concludes his last letter with the impassioned plea, "Amen, amen, for love, amen!"

CHAPTER 9

John Ball and Wat Tyler

JOHN BALL provided the inspiration behind the Peasants' Revolt. His sympathy, his understanding, and his enthusiasm combined to create a driving force which was easily communicated to the people. But he needed organisational support, and this was given to him by a fellow citizen of Colchester, named Wat Tyler.

Here again, we find that confusion has arisen over the origin of this particular Walter who practised his trade as a tiler within Colchester's hallowed walls. So many history books have continued to refer to Wat Tyler as a man of Kent. This incorrect tradition has been so firmly established that inns in the county have been named after him, and country lanes have borne his title for some considerable time.

Further misunderstanding has occurred from the fact that there was a John Tyler of Dartford in Kent, who, when a government tax collector, insisting that his daughter was over fifteen years of age and therefore liable for Poll Tax, began an indecent examination of the girl, slew the man in defence of his daughter's honour. This incident sparked off the rising in that area, and is reported by Stowe in his *Annales*. This man was often confused with Wat Tyler, and I have seen a recent article in a popular history magazine where the incident is transferred to Brentwood in Essex, and the man's name given as Walter Tyler, the peasant leader!

But the evidence of reputable historians is quite definite on the point. Charles Oman refers to a description of him in a contemporary Maidstone document as "Walter Tyler of Colchester" who was chosen chief at that town.[1] Trial juries of

---

[1] Op. cit., p. 36.

Faversham and Downingford in Kent describe him as "Walterum Teghler de Essex"[1] and the chronicle *Eulogium Historiarum* calls him "Unus tegulator de Estex".

Hilton and Fagan state categorically that "Tyler, too came from Colchester, the home of John Ball, and it would seem likely that he had been influenced by the preaching of Ball".[2] Similarly, Lindsay and Groves report that Tyler lived in Colchester, must have heard Ball speak, and was possibly converted by him.[3]

It is Dr Kriehn who sums it all up most emphatically when he writes:–

> "The identity of Tyler is established beyond a doubt by the Kentish jury indictments. The jurymen of Maidstone, where he was elected captain, would certainly have known whether he was their fellow townsman, and they distinctly inform us that he was from Colchester. This statement finds confirmation in two other indictments taken at the same time by men of the county through which he passed, viz: those of Faversham and Downhamford, which tell us that he was an Essex man. Our chain of evidence is completed by the statement of a reliable contemporary chronicler to the effect that a tiler of Essex was spokesman of the insurgents at Blackheath".[4]

The reason for Wat Tyler being at Maidstone in Kent at the beginning of the Revolt has puzzled some historians. Both Anthony Steel and Sir James Ramsey explain this by saying he was an Essex man settled in Kent. But a study of all the evidence points to the fact that Tyler, marching from Colchester to London with the Essex men, left the main body, and, with a small band, crossed the Thames at Tilbury and hastened to Maidstone where he released John Ball imprisoned in the Archbishop of Canterbury's gaol there for the past month. Tyler was then elected leader of the Kent men, and with Ball, marched with them on London, south of the river. For this reason, therefore, his name has been associated with Kent.

---

[1] *Archaeologica Cantiana*, iii, 92–3.
[2] Op. cit., p. 103.
[3] Op. cit.
[4] Op. cit., p. 459.

44

Wat Tyler had seen service in the French wars, serving under Richard Lyons, Sergeant-at-Arms to Edward III. Quick-witted, self-reliant and ambitious, Wat was a powerful speaker and an able negotiator. He had learned much from his military service abroad, and modern historians pay tribute to him as a good military strategist, showing wisdom and ability as a leader, exercising restraint on the side of discipline.

Back in England, with his French war scars, he was plying his trade as a tiler in his home town of Colchester. Inevitably he came into contact with John Ball.

But, of course, the monks had no good word to say for Wat. One monkish writer describes him as "a crafty fellow of an excellent wit, but lacking grace". Walsingham says he was "a cunning man endowed with much sense if he had decided to apply his intelligence to good purpose."

The relationship of the two men was ideal. John Ball was the heart, and Wat Tyler the head, of the insurrection.

These two, the chaplain and the tiler, had a clear idea of what they were striving for. They wished to abolish intermediary power – the lawyers, aldermen, guildsmen, churchmen, town monopolists, lords and nobles – and to create an England of peasants, craftsmen and workers – free and equal, with a monarchy resting on popular support.

The project was clearly to set up a new order to things, founded on social equality. This is a theory which, in the whole history of the Middle Ages, appears for the first and last time in connection with this Revolt.

In order to achieve this, John Ball and Wat Tyler together created an organisation, an underground movement among the people, which they built up throughout Eastern England. It was known, as we have seen, as "Magna Societas" – "The Great Society".

In an interesting and informative study of the culture of this period in our history, *Chaucer in His Time*, the author, Derek Brewer, writes of the Peasants' Revolt,

> "For all their absurdities, the English peasants, when driven to revolt, had a constructive plan of society, and, for all their violence, showed a sense of direction and a degree of responsibility that compares favourably with the much

worse uprisings of the worst oppressed peasants in France".

CHAPTER 10

Chronicles of The Revolt

THE contemporary sources from which information about the Peasants' Revolt may be obtained are, of course, the chroniclers, the historians of that period. There are a number of these who have included, in their histories, some account of the dramatic happenings in the early summer of 1381 which became known as "The Hurling Time".

The best known, and most often quoted chronicle was that of Jean Froissart, Latin secretary to Queen Phillipa, wife of Edward III. A burgher's son from Valenciennes, from an early age he was determined to be a historian, and his talent for facile expression made his *Chroniques* one of the classics of Middle French literature. But admirable as Froissart's account of the Revolt may be from a poetical point of view, it is very little use from an historical one. He was not an eye-witness of the events in England in 1381 and his information about them was obtained solely by interviews. He studied no documents, and his writings do not show the influence of an well-informed eye-witness. Throughout, he shows a love and admiration for the chivalry of his age, and is obviously a historian of the upper classes. His purpose in writing was to act as a warning, to show the sin and folly of such a rebellion, and to exalt the heroism of the nobility, especially that of the young King. He is never fair to rebels, and refers to the whole revolt as a "pestillensse". All through his history, he expressed the opinion that the common people are fools who rebel because they are too prosperous and don't know what they want. They are led by men who are rogues and scalawags. His estimate of the relative worth of the classes in England is contained in the following words:–

"Li gentilhomme sont de noble et loial condition, et li

communs peuples est de fele, perilleas, orgueilleuse et desloiale condition."

It is unfortunate that Froissart has been so much quoted, in standard English history books, as a source of information about the Peasants' Revolt. This has, for many years, coloured our view of this stirring event in our history. And, in erroneously describing John Ball as "a mad priest from Kent", he has distorted and denigrated this great English folk hero.

A classic example of this distortion of historical fact is found in the charming narrative embodying the traditional view of the meeting of King Richard II and the people at Mile End, found in J. R. Green's *History of the English People*:–

"On the morning of the 14th therefore, Richard rode from the Tower to Mile End, to meet the Essex men. 'I am your King and lord, good people', the boy began, with the fearlessness which marked his bearing throughout the crisis, 'What will you?'. 'We will that you free us forever', shouted the peasants, 'us and our lands, and that we be never named nor held for serfs'. 'I grant it', replied Richard; and he bade them go home, pledging himself at once to issue charters of freedom and amnesty. A shout of joy welcomed the promise. Throughout the day more than thirty clerks were busy writing letters of pardon and emancipation, and with these, the mass of the Essex men and the men of Hertfordshire withdrew quietly to their homes."

This extract is based entirely on Froissart, being simply an abbreviation of his narrative. How completely incorrect this is will be shown later, but this sort of thing is, unhappily, still being taught in History lessons in our schools.

Some other chroniclers are also unreliable. *Chronicon Angliae* covering 1328–1388 and written by Thomas Walsingham, a monk of St. Albans Abbey, is a most interesting account and the longest contemporary narrative. But he was influenced mainly by the local happenings at St. Albans, and his record of the London events is somewhat inaccurate. His is not the work of a particularly conscientious chronicler, and he always shows the insurgents in the worst possible light.

Evesham's Chronicle for the period 1377–1402, written by a monk from Evesham, appears to share a common source with Walsingham. A study of this monk's works, sometimes referred to under the title, *Vita Ricardi II,* gives the impression that this is in no way a contemporary account, but that the author was using many previously published sources.

The *Polychronicon,* written by Ralph Higden, a monk of Westminster, between the years 1432 and 1450, is, apparently, partly based on the *Evesham Chronicle,* but some of it reads like the work of an eye-witness. But *Knighton's Chronicle,* the work of Henry Knighton, a canon of St. Mary's Abbey, Leicester, would seem to consist almost entirely of hearsay evidence.

The most reliable of the chronicles are two in number, the *Anonimalle Chronicle,* and the *Eulogium Historiarum.*

The *Anonimalle Chronicle,* covering the years 1333–1381 is attributed to an anonymous monk from St. Mary's Abbey, York, and penned not more than a year or two after the Revolt. It is written in French, but is evidently the work of an Englishman. It is considered to be the single most important source for the history of the Rising. The events in Kent, Essex and London are minutely and vividly described as one would expect from an eye-witness, and the author bears every mark of being a contemporary. George Kriehn considers this chronicle to be the most valuable of the surviving contemporary accounts of the Revolt.

The *Continuation of the Eulogium Historiarum Sine Temporis* is the work of an unknown author who may have been a monk of Cantebury. It covers the period 1364–1413, and the narrative is independent of all known chroniclers. It is a continuation of a previous well-known compendium of history extending till 1366, and one of several others published. Its statements are confirmed by other chroniclers, and, again, Kriehn considers this to be one of the most reliable contemporary sources.

So, from this collection of medieval chroniclers of the Peasants' Revolt, we find that there are **two** that can be relied upon to give a reasonably correct picture of what happened in 1381. It must be remembered, however, that the authors of both the *Anonimalle* and the *Eulogium* were probably monks who, because of their position in the established Church order, would not be entirely sympathetic to any revolt which was directed very largely against the Church itself. This is not necessarily so in the case of all monks, and, in the work of these two authors, we certainly do not find the bitter hatred and scorn towards the common people as is shown in the chronicles of Froissart and Walsingham.

We can, therefore, safely use the testimony given in the *Anonimalle* and the *Eulogium* in any account of this great Peasants' Revolt of 1381, as modern historians are now beginning to do.

CHAPTER 11

Protagonists in the Drama

TWO of the main characters in the Revolt, John Ball and Wat Tyler, have already been given detailed mention. Reference to some of the other chief actors in this great drama can now be made, in order to get a better understanding of its unfolding. For, through the interaction of the personalities of the protagonists in this 1381 struggle, the shape of things to come began to emerge.

RICHARD II (1367–1400) the young, newly-crowned, inexperienced King of but fifteen years of age, was an important figure, even if more a 'figure-head' than an actual person in his own right. Neither by natural disposition, nor by youth training, was he well fitted to be a king. He had been brought up among the ladies of the Court, and was dominated by his mother, widow of the Black Prince, his father. He was already showing signs of a neurotic temperament which developed in later life. He was quick-tempered, indulged in gusts of passion, was abrupt in manner, and stammered slightly. He loved fine clothes, and spent great sums on pomp and ceremony. His own suits of clothing cost him £1000 a garment. He is credited with the invention of the handkerchief, for his own and Court use. In all, he was a weak and vicious character, turning night into day with drinking bouts and indulging in unnatural vice. His personal friend and confidant, Robert de Vere, Earl of Oxford, might be considered in several respects as a second Piers Gaveston. Richard had to face many problems when he came to the throne, as his grandfather, Edward III, certainly left him a "damnosa haereditas". But, in tackling this, he showed no signs of courage or clear-sighted action, nor did he demand independence of the Council.

JOAN OF KENT (1328–1385), widow of the celebrated Edward the Black Prince, son and heir of Edward III, she was a dominating person during this period of the Revolt. A notable beauty in her youth, known as "the Fair Maid of Kent", she had earlier become involved with the young Earl of Salisbury, contracting a marriage with him, and then getting wed to Sir Thomas Holland who went to the wars and got killed. A widow for the first time, she turned from her first lover, Salisbury, and married Edward the Black Prince, a reputedly love match on both sides. An ageing woman of over fifty years of age, still possessing a strong animal magnetism, she had two recorded personal contacts with the rebels, escaping, on both occasions, with nothing more harmful than a few kisses from enthusiastic insurgents. She owned manors in twenty-six counties, most of them in Lincolnshire.

ARCHBISHOP SIMON OF SUDBURY, born in Sudbury, Suffolk, was consecrated Archbishop in 1375. He was a learned, eloquent and liberal prelate, lacking independence of character but ambitious for both the Church and himself. He was given the additional post of Chancellor in January 1380 – "whether he sought the post of his own free will, or had it thrust upon him by others, only God can tell" – the author of the *Chronicon Angliae* comments. The archbishop was a pious, well-intentioned man, within his limits, but somewhat indecisive in manner and destitute of firmness and tact. The main criticism of him by the chroniclers was that he was too lenient to heretics. He was a half-hearted prosecutor of John Ball, which accounts partly for the latter's long period of roaming at will around Colchester. Simon's skull, with the large gash in it over the eye socket, providing evidence of his dreadful death, may be seen in the vestry of St. Gregory's Church, Sudbury, adjoining which once stood the small cottage where he was born.

WILLIAM WALWORTH, LORD MAYOR OF LONDON (d. 1385). A City merchant engaged in the fish trade, William Walworth was the most eminent member of the Fishmongers Guild in London. A shrewd, able and determined businessman, he was involved in all the consultations and negotiations which took place during the days of revolt. He acted with vigour throughout, and was subsequently rewarded by a knighthood by King Richard, at first protesting that he was a mere merchant unworthy to have and maintain a knight's estate, but eventually being persuaded to accept it.

JACK STRAW. One of the notable rebel leaders in Essex, he has sometimes been referred to as the Jack Rackstraw mentioned in some of the chronicles, and it has also been suggested that his was merely a nickname for Wat Tyler. But the Rolls of Parliament of 1381, the primary authority of all, clearly distinguish Tyler and Straw as two separate persons. There is a strong tradition that he was the rector of Fobbing in Essex and this is likely, as Fobbing was one of the militant Essex villages, being the first to start the Revolt, and producing another well-known leader in Thomas Baker, the village baker, the first identifiable rebel of 1381. Lindsay and Groves refer to Straw as the parish priest of Fobbing, the most important captain of the rebels next to Ball and Tyler. Other authorities have mentioned his clerical connection with Fobbing but, as the parish records are not available as far back as 1381, it is not possible to get confirmation from this source. From his conduct as a leader during the Revolt, Straw was obviously a man of some organisational ability, for he took charge of the Essex force when Tyler moved over into Kent.

SIR ROBERT HALES, Master of the Order of the Knights of St. John, the Knights Hospitallers, was the Treasurer of England during the Revolt. Following the failure of the 1379 Graduated Poll Tax, which was a reasonably fair one, he introduced the iniquitous Poll Tax of 1380 which bore heavily on the peasants. For this, he was universally hated and became known as 'Hobbe the Robber'. From all reports he was a hard, unyielding man who had a little sympathy with the plight of the people. He farmed out the tax collection in many cases, and employed a number of Commissioners who used very dubious methods in order to obtain the taxes.

WILLIAM COURTENAY, BISHOP OF LONDON (1342–1396). In 1375, Courtenay became bishop of England's capital city. He was a man of principle, a constitutional churchman who laboured for the welfare and good government of the Church. He was not aligned with any particular political faction, or indulged in political intrigue. He never strayed from his duty to the Church, and, in 1377, he showed this by his involvement in a dispute with John of Gaunt over the trial of John Wycliffe.

HENRY LE DESPENSER, BISHOP OF NORWICH (1341–1406). Grandson of Hugh le Despenser, one of the favourites of Edward II, Despenser was a soldier rather than a churchman. An arrogant and headstrong noble, he was constantly involved in disputes with the people in his diocese. In 1377, he had a long row with the townsfolk of Lynn over the carrying of the town's mace before him, a privilege previously reserved for the Mayor. When the Peasants' Revolt broke out, he was at his manor of Burleigh in Rutland, and this gave him the opportunity of resuming his military character. His subsequent action played a decisive part in the happenings in that area.

WILLIAM MONTAGUE, EARL OF SALISBURY (1328–1397). An experienced soldier and politican, he saw service with Edward, the Black Prince, in the wars in France, commanding one of the wings at Poitiers, with great credit to himself. As a young man, he exchanged a marriage contract with Joan, the Fair Maid of Kent, but this was annulled when she married Sir Thomas Holland. During the Revolt, Salisbury was with the King in the Tower of London, and, at the negotiations with the rebels, his advice was always on the side of moderation.

SIR ROBERT KNOLLES (1317–1407). An old 'condottiere', Sir Robert was a professional soldier, skilled and experienced. In 1357, he was plundering Normandy at the head of a force known as "The Great Company". In 1381, he was in London at his house in the city with one hundred and twenty men-at-arms and archers guarding the wealth he had accummulated there. As the Revolt developed, he took charge of the London Citizen Army, and played a vital role in the concluding days. Subsequently, he was awarded the manor of St. Pancras by a grateful King Richard.

SIR ROBERT TRESILIAN (d. 1388). A Cornishman, as his name suggests, Sir Robert came to London and rapidly achieved success in the legal profession, soon becoming a judge. He was noted for his severity in dealing with wrongdoers. On the 22nd June, 1381, he was created Chief Justice of the King's Bench, and, as such, was involved in the legal actions that followed the collapse of the Revolt. Chronicler Knighton refers to him as being active everywhere and sparing no one. It was alleged that he was a worshipper of demons.

CHAPTER 12

The Start of the Rising

THE *Enclyclopedia Britannica* describes the Peasants' Revolt of 1381 as the first great popular rebellion in English history. The Poll Tax of that year had brought to a head a fund of economic discontent which had been growing since the middle of the century. The Revolt drew support from several sources, not only the peasants but master-craftsmen, small merchants, well-to-do artisans, the poorer clergy, and even some of the county knights, were found in its ranks. Thus, some historians have refused to call it the Peasants' Revolt, but refer to it as a "Rising" (Powell), "Great Revolt" (Charles Oman), "English Rising" (Hilton and Fagan) or, more explicitly, "Social Revolt" (Kriehn). For the social tensions that were building up for over half a century had to find expression.

The most important cause of tension was, undoubtedly, the hated Poll Tax of 1381. A shilling (3 groats) a head represented three days wages, so a family of four adults would have to pay twelve days wages in tax. There were, also, serious shortcomings in the collection of this tax. Consequently, some ministers, seeing that the collectors had failed, bought up the right to collect the balance, and, by pressing the peasants hard, hoped to make a nice profit for themselves. Chronicler Knighton reports that some tax commissioners took to examining young girls to see if they were virgins. If this was not obvious, then they were taxed as adults irrespective of age. Royal writs for all this were issued throughout Kent and Essex.

Contemporary writers have admitted that this tax placed a larger share of the burden upon the very poor. The author of the *Anonimalle Chronicle* comments that many lords and commons thought the tax was unfairly levied from the poor and not from the rich, and that, in any case, the collectors had retained most of the yield.

As is often the case in many other aspects of life, it was but a small incident which sparked the whole thing off. The catalyst which caused the great Peasant's Revolt to come to a boil was the determination of the inhabitants of three Essex villages to band together and refuse to pay the Poll Tax. The people of Corringham, Fobbing and Stanford-le-Hope, marshland communities on the Thames Estuary, were not going to endure any more of this deliberate piece of class legislation. "Tax has tenet us alle!" they complained. So, they withheld payment.

Consequently, on the 30th May, Tax Commissioner, Thomas Bampton, rode out into Essex to deal with this matter of tax default. With him were three clerks and two sergeants-at-arms. He made for the town of Brentwood where he had ordered the headmen of the defaulting villages to appear before him.

It was unfortunate for the Commissioner that he had selected Fobbing as one of the first places to be dealt with. For this was a particularly militant village. Led by Thomas Baker, the village baker, Jack Straw, the rector, and supported by William Gildbourne, a wealthy landowner, the villagers turned up en masse and hit back. Thomas Bampton and his five supporters were overwhelmed, beaten up, unceremoniously thrown on to their horses, and driven out of the town back to London.

Chronicler Knighton describes Thomas Baker's action in the following terms:—

> "Thomas Baker of Fobbing (so called because of this trade) took courage and began to make speeches and to find supporters among some of the men of the villages. Then, others joined them, and then each of them sent messages to their friends and relatives, and so further, from village to village, district to district, seeking advice and asking them to bring prompt help with respect to those needs which they had in common, and which bore so heavily on them. And they began to gather together in companies with great show of jubilation, as was their wont". (*Chronicon II, p. 131*)

On Whitsunday, June 2nd, the authorities made a quick

counter-move. Sir Robert Belknap, Chief Justice of Common Pleas, together with twenty helmeted and lightly-armoured soldiers, and the three same clerks as before, moved out to Brentwood on a Commission of Trailbaston to seek out and punish the rioters. Commissions of Trailbaston, visitations by judges sent by the King to put down robbers and thugs (those who carried sticks of "bastons"), were much hated by the people as, owing to false indictments presented by jurors, they did more harm to the innocent than to the guilty.

Faced with an even larger crowd of rebels, many of them well armed, Sir Robert stood a slimmer chance than his predecessor. He was, likewise, ignominiously defeated, after his three clerks, and six local jurors he had sworn in, were killed.

The Revolt now spread like wildfire. On hearing the news from Brentwood, Wat Tyler moved quickly. He had to take charge as his fellow conspirator, John Ball, had been arrested a month earlier and was confined in the Archbishop's prison at Maidstone. But Wat received plenty of local support. It is, recorded that William Roger, of South Ockendon, and John Smith, of Rainham, rode around, giving the signal for the rising. As did Henry Baker, of Manningtree.

Colchester, where it had all been planned, was entered on Tuesday, June 4th. A higher proportion of men from that town, than from any other, joined the ranks of the rebel army. Nowhere else in the area had such support been given.

Wat was ably supported by Jack Straw, the Fobbing incumbent, and, as the Revolt gained strength, much of this was due to the fact that a number of educated men were available as its leaders, and among these were found many of the country clergy.

Records are available which list the following local priests among those who took an active part in the rising:— John Ball, chaplain of Colchester; Jack Straw, rector of Fobbing, in Essex; John Wrawe, rector of Ringsfield; John Smith, rector of Stansfield; Walter, incumbent of Ixworth; the vicar of Mildenhall; Geoffrey Parfreye, vicar of All Saints', Sudbury, and his chaplain Thomas; John Battisford, rector of Bucklesham; and Nicolas Bacon and John Oxenford, chantry priests from Clare; all in Suffolk. John Michel, a chaplain from

Ely, also played a prominent part.

Among lay supporters were James de Bedingfield and Thomas Sampson of Harkstead. Some country gentry did support the Revolt for personal and discreditable reasons, but many of them felt a genuine animosity against the incompetent, selfish and corrupt ministers of the King.

Writing in the *Transactions of the Essex Archaeological Society* on the subject of "Essex in Insurrection, 1381", published in Colchester in 1878, J. A. Sparvel-Bayly makes this observation,

"It is indeed more than probable that if the rebellion begun by peasants and shoeless vagabonds had not been so soon quelled, persons of a higher class, like the esquire (Armiger) Bertram de Wilmyngtone of Kent, might have undertaken the conduct of it, and effected its object."

News of the Essex happenings soon spread over the river to Kent. A contemporary writer reported that "when the men of Kent heard the news of what they had long hoped for, they rose and joined in". Led by Robert Cave (another baker) of Dartford, and John Hales of Malling, they now began to organise for a march on London. Among the clergy supporting them was William, chaplain at St. John's Church in Thanet.

Wat Tyler, with Jack Straw, led the Essex men out of Colchester on to the London road. But Wat knew that he would have to leave them before he reached the capital, in order to rescue John Ball from his sojourn in Maidstone gaol. When arrested a month previously, John had said that he would soon be released by twenty thousand armed men. Wat was determined to see that this prophecy came true.

CHAPTER 13

The March on London

LEAVING the Essex men under Jack Straw at Romford, Wat Tyler, with a score of so of picked men, rode rapidly to Tilbury. On the morning of June 7th, he crossed the Thames and pressed on to Maidstone. Here he met the Kent Rebels and together they released John Ball from the Archbishop's prison, the Kent force numbering at that time approximately twenty thousand men, the number that the priest had prophesied would come to his rescue.

Rochester Castle had been stormed by the insurgents on the previous day, in order to release the serf from Gravesend who had been publicly arrested and imprisoned there by Sir Simon Burley, a close adviser to the King.

The rebel army moved on to Canterbury on June 10th. The town gave them a rapturous welcome. With John Ball at their head, they entered the cathedral at mid-day, seeking the Archbishop for a confrontation. Mass was being said, and the terrified monks reported that he was not there, having fled to London the previous day. The rebels thereupon ordered the monks to elect John Ball as a new archbishop, but he was able to persuade them that this could not be done in that way.

The march on London was then decided on, and the rebel force of Kentish men had now increased to about fifty thousand. In good order and with excellent discipline, this large force started off on its seventy mile journey to London. They wanted, as they said, to see the King, and to tell him certain things.

A misplaced faith in the young King was one of the characteristics of the Revolt. The rebels believed that the monarch was an institution standing above individuals and classes, capable of dispensing even-handed justice. They were soon to be sadly disillusioned. But to Richard they were determined to go in order to obtain some remedy for their grievances. It was, they thought, his evil ministers who were standing in the way, preventing justice from coming to the common people. If they could only get to the King himself, they would persuade him of the righteousness of their cause.

With this object in view, they marched forward with confidence. Wat Tyler kept a firm grip on his men. His military genius was never shown to better advantage than on this celebrated march. To weld a mob of over fifty thousand into a disciplined force and control them on this long trek was a feat which indicated clearly the outstanding character of this rebel leader. His orders to the rebels under his command were firm and to the point:–

"Remember, men, we come not as thieves and robbers. We come seeking social justice!"

These words set the whole tone of the hazardous enterprise. Wat Tyler kept in touch with the Essex men north of the river who had resumed their march on London. Their numbers were almost similar to those of the Kent men, the combined army being, therefore, a considerable force to control in these or any other times.

Some critics have queried the chroniclers' estimates of the numbers of the rebels, put at about sixty thousand each for the Essex and Kent contingents. These figures seem to be agreed in reports such as those of the author of the *Anonimalle,* and Froissart. Walsingham reports the number as two hundred thousand listening to John Ball 'corrupting them with his doctrine' but this, coming from a writer bitterly antagonistic to the aims of the insurgents, may be taken as a deliberate exaggeration in order to make the Revolt appear more terrifying.

The figure that John Ball suggested would be available to rescue him from prison could be taken as a low estimate, but, as the march progressed, many more rebels joined on the way, and, therefore, the number of fifty thousand might be established as a fair assessment.

In answer to the criticism that such large numbers could not be gathered together in any confined space, the reply could be made that many of us took part in gatherings in London, as large, or even larger, than those in 1381, when over one hundred thousand people were safely assembled in Trafalgar Square, on a number of Mondays, in the late 1950's and 1960's.

As the march towards London continued, an incident occurred on the 11th June, as they neared the village of Eltham. A small group of travellers was seen emerging from a side road which also led to Canterbury. It consisted of a gaily painted whirlcote (a covered carriage of the period), accompanied by a score or so of servants and men-at-arms. In it reclined the King's mother, the celebrated 'Fair Maid of Kent', returning from a pilgrimage to the tomb of her late husband, the Black Prince.

The rebels offered no harm to the Princess Joan, for they held her son in respect, and were actually on the way to put their grievances before him. From what can be gathered from the reports, they were in high spirits, and expressed humour towards the Princess and her female attendants which was typically bawdy but friendly. Froissart, who could not imagine that these rustics could be anything but menacing towards members of the royalty, gives a typical report that "these people came to her chare, and dealt rudely with her, whereof the good lady was in great doubt but they would have done some villainy to her or to her damosels. Howbeit, God kept her, and she came in one day from Canterbury to London."

Froissart, of course, got this story from someone he interviewed after the event. It is doubtful if John Ball, with all the cares of this great Revolt on his mind, or Wat Tyler, who served under the Black Prince in France, would have allowed petty insults to be directed towards the mother of their King. They had other and more lofty objects in view.

The Kent men pressed on and reached Blackheath early on the evening of June 12th, the eve of the Festival of Corpus Christi. Before they settled down for the night on the Common, three horsemen arrived from London with a message from the King. They were Aldermen of the city, members of the Fishmongers Guild, John Horne, Adam Carlyle and John Fresch. They reported that King Richard had sent them to find out the purpose of this great assembly. Wat told the Aldermen that they came seeking justice, and wished to express their grievances to the King personally. The Aldermen replied that, if they would all return to their homes, the King would consider the matter. This answer was not considered satisfactory by the rebel leaders. As the three messengers were mounting up preparatory to riding back to London, Alderman Horne, a secret supporter of the Revolt, whispered to Wat that the London people were ready to receive and welcome the insurgent army, and that the London Bridge gate would be open to them.

Fortified by this assurance, the rebel army settled down quietly for the night on Blackheath Common.

But, before they got their rest, the Royal Barge was reported to be slowly coming down the Thames to Greenwich. King Richard was apparently desirous of having some parley with his rebellious subjects. The barge remained in mid-stream while the insurgents gathered on the bank to see what was going to happen. King Richard was seen on the prow, arguing with his Chancellor, Archbishop Simon, and his Treasurer, Sir Robert Hales. Then, after some hesitation, the barge turned round and went back to London. The author of the *Anonimalle Chronicle* explained this strange action in the following terms:–

"On the Wednesday (i.e. on 12th June), being in the Tower of London and deciding to deal with this matter, the King had his barges got ready and took with him in his own barge, the Archbishop, Treasurer and certain others of his Council. Accompanied by four other barges for his men, he travelled to Greenwich, three leagues from London. But there the said Chancellor and Treasurer informed the King that it would be too great folly to go to the commons, for they were unreasonable men and did not know how to behave".[1]

---

[1] Op. cit., pp. 133–140.

CHAPTER 14

John Ball's Sermon at Blackheath

EARLY next morning, with the sun shining brightly, John Ball celebrated Mass on Blackheath Common before a concourse of over fifty thousand armed and resolute men, setting up his little altar on a small hillock known to this day as "Tyler's Mount". It was the Festival day of thanksgiving for the institution of the Holy Eucharist by Christ, and, on this occasion, he preached a sermon which has come down through six hundred years as the most moving plea for social equality in the history of the English language.

Allowing for the fact that the record of this was made by contemporary writers of the period who were bitter opponents of the man who preached it, namely chroniclers Froissart and Walsingham, and that it was delivered over six hundred years ago, when men and women were treated like animals by those in authority and when human life had little value, it is certainly a remarkable homily, looked at from any point of view. The priest who created it was, obviously, a remarkable man, who, in those far-off, unenlightened days, saw a dignity in men and women, hitherto unrealised, but which, with the right will and determination, could be achieved, if they stood together and asserted it.

Froissart quotes it thus:–

"Ah, ye good people, the matters goeth not well to pass in England, nor shall do till everything be common, and there be no villeins or gentlemen, but that we may be all united together, and that the lords be no greater masters than we be. What have we deserved, or why should we be kept thus in servage? We be all come from one father and one mother, Adam and Eve; whereby can they say or show that they be greater lords than we be, saving by that they cause us to win and labour for that they dispend?

"They are clothed in velvet and camlet furred with grise, and we be vestured with poor cloth: they have their wines, spices and good bread, and we have the drawing out of the chaff and drink water; they dwell in fair houses, and we have the pain and travail, rain and wind in the fields; and, by that that cometh of our labours, they keep and maintain their estates; we be called their bondmen, and, without we do readily them service, we are beaten; and we have no sovereign to whom we may complain, nor that will hear us nor do us right.

"Let us go to the King, he is young, and show him what servage we be in, and show him how we will have it otherwise, or else we will provide us of some remedy; and if we go together, all manner of people that now be in bondage will follow us to the intent to be made free; and when the King seeth, we shall have some remedy, either by fairness or otherwise."

Walsingham, in his *Chronicon Angliae*, adds the following about this particular sermon of Ball's:

"And to corrupt more people with his doctrine, at Blackheath, where two hundred thousand of the commons were gathered together, he began a sermon in this fashion:

'When Adam dalf and Eve span,
who was thanne a gentilman?'

"And continuing his sermon, he tried to prove by the words of the proverb that he had taken for his text, that, from the beginning all men were created equal by nature, and that servitude had been introduced by the unjust and evil oppression of men, against the will of God, who, if it had pleased Him to create serfs, surely in the beginning of the world would have appointed who should be a serf and who a lord.

"Let them consider, therefore, that he had now appointed the time wherein, laying aside the yoke of long servitude, they might, if they wished, enjoy their liberty so long desired. Wherefore they must be prudent, hastening to act after the manner of a good husbandman, tilling his field, and uprooting the tares that are accustomed to destroy the grain; first killing the great lords of the realm, then slaying the lawyers, justices and jurors and, finally, rooting out everyone whom they knew to be harmful to the community in future.

"So, at last, they would obtain peace and security, if, when the great ones had been removed, they maintained among themselves equality of liberty and nobility, as well as of dignity and power."

In this celebrated sermon, John Ball shows that he rejected entirely any idea of achieving a social balance or relationship between the lords and serfs, a view held by many previous Christian writers. But his reported incentive to a general massacre of evil lords may be treated with a certain amount of caution, written as it was by a monk of St. Albans who was well-known for his inaccuracies in reporting the London events, and, for his antagonism to everything the rebels stood for.

But Ball does emphasise clearly the fact, not entirely realised in his day, that it was due to the hard work of the peasants that the lords were enabled to live the luxurious lives they did. And, with unerring logic and devastating simplicity, he points out that, if God had wanted there to be class distinctions, he would surely have created them in the beginning!

Hints of Ball's millenarian views, seen in four of his six letters,[1] are again found in this sermon when he re-affirms that God has now appointed the time for the great changes that were coming to pass. In this, he was in line with the apocalyptic visions of the end of an existing order and the creation of a new one, in which men now living could take an active part, which were found all over Europe, particularly after the thirteenth century. These were, at the time, unknown in England, and this fact gives this sermon such an effective impact.

Shortly after the conclusion of John Ball's sermon, the Royal Barge again wended its way downstream to the open fields of the royal manor of Rotherhythe, just above Blackheath. On

---

[1] Previously quoted in Chapter 8.

board were again King Richard and his ministers, the latter bent on urging the King to try to come to some terms with the rebels. Standing on the prow of his vessel, Richard called to the assembled crowd on the bank and asked them what they wanted. They replied that Richard should come ashore, and they would discuss with him the things they lacked.

Richard's ministers were terrified that, if he went ashore to confer with the rebels, they might lose him, their trump card. After further heated discussion on board, the Earl of Salisbury, one of the King's advisers, and an ex-lover of his mother, pushed himself forward and decided the issue with the words to the rebels, "Sirs, ye be not in such order nor array that the King ought to speak with you!".[1]

With this disdainful expression, the Earl indicated clearly the superior self-esteem and self-satisfaction of the nobility who, even when faced with a revolt of the people which threatened their whole existence, would not deign to allow their monarch to have discussion with those who were not properly arrayed or not presenting themselves in the proper manner, fit for the occasion.

King Richard and his party returned to the safety of the Tower of London, and the rebel army moved on towards the capital. They were now in close contact with their Essex comrades north of the river. These had received further support from a London goldsmith, Thomas Farringdon, who had ridden out to meet them. Although his father was a bastard, Farringdon bore the surname of one of the most famous of medieval London families. He is still remembered today by a well-known street in the city which is named after him.

Together with Jack Straw, Henry Baker, Adam Michel, John Kyrkeby and John Starling, Essex men who were emerging as leaders of this large concourse of rebels, Farringdon took his part in their organisation as they approached London. On June 12th, their main body lay encamped in the fields at Mile End, outside the north-east corner of the city walls. A number of local clergy had, apparently, joined them as André Reville reports that many chaplains and parish priests had to fly and go into

---

[1] Froissart *Chroniques X*, pp. 97–107.

hiding when the insurrection was over.[1]

Thus, on the morning of the Festival of Corpus Christi in the year 1381, these two great armies of resolute Englishmen, from Essex in the north, and Kent in the east, numbering over one hundred thousand men, were poised ready to descend on their capital and confront their King and his ministers with their just demands. London, with a population of a mere thirty thousand, awaited expectantly, its workers optimistic and eager, its rulers pessimistic and fearful.

---

[1] *Le Soulevement des Travailleurs d'Angleterre en 1381.* Ed. Charles Petit – Dutaillis, *Societe de l'Ecole des Chartes.* Paris 1898, p. 225.

CHAPTER 15

London Entered

LATER that morning, the men of Kent moved on to London. As they approached Southwark and London Bridge, they were met by Alderman John Horne who assured them that they would find none but friends in London, and that a fellow-alderman, Walter Sibley, another sympathiser, had lowered the drawbridge ready for their entry. On the previous evening, scouting parties had found the drawbridge raised on the news of their aproach, and had to be content with breaking open two prisons in Southwark, the Marshalsea and the King's Bench, releasing the prisoners. But, now the way was apparently open for the rebels to enter the town with many ready to receive them.

Before crossing London Bridge, the insurgents stopped in order to destroy the London brothels at Southwark, close by the Bridge. In medieval times, the brothel area of any town had to be outside the city walls. This was so, for example, in Colchester, where it was situated in Vineyard Street, under the south walls of the town. Christian city inhabitants in fourteenth century England could only sleep happily in their beds at night with the knowledge that any fornication that was taking place was occurring outside their hallowed walls. And the prostitutes were also forbidden to live within the towns. Any caught there at night were fined and escorted back to their authorised area, sometimes headed by a piper playing a suitable lament.

It is not surprising, therefore, that the insurgents went straight for the Southwark brothels, and burnt them to the ground. They had done the same in Colchester, destroying the Vineyard Street area, before leaving, a few days previously. It is known that John Ball had, in his preaching, expressed some strict views about morality, saying on one occasion, that no one born out of wedlock had a right to hold an official position in the Church. It can be assumed, therefore, that he would be one of the initiators of this destruction of the houses of ill repute at Southwark.

The *Anonimalle Chronicle* reports the incident as follows:–

"And on the same day of Corpus Christi, in the morning, the commons of Kent broke down a brothel (une measone destrves), near London Bridge, occupied by Flemish women, who had leased it from the Mayor of London".[1]

The Lord Mayor of London at this time was a certain William Walworth, who was running a very profitable business, importing Flemish girls from the Continent into these Southwark houses which he had leased from their owner, William of Wykeham, Bishop of Winchester.[2]

That afternoon, the Kent rebels entered London, and marched along Bridge Street to the tumultuous shouts of the inhabitants. They soon made contact with their comrades from Essex, who had been let into the city through the Ald Gate by another alderman sympathiser, William Tonge.

Historians, on the whole, have been critical of the action of a number of London aldermen, John Horne, Adam Carlisle, John Fresch, Walter Sibley and William Tonge, who, by opening the various gates, enabled the rebels from both Essex and Kent to enter London without any difficulty. Charles Oman refers to them in the headlines, "THE TRAITOR ALDERMEN", and R. B. Dobson describes their activities as "THE TREACHERY OF LONDON ALDERMEN". But the contemporary chroniclers, strangely enough, do not mention the activity of these men at all. The *Anonimalle* merely states that, as a result of the clamour of the rebels, the gatekeepers let them in. The aldermen are only mentioned, after the revolt, in the Inquisitions held before the London Sheriffs in November of 1381. Their actions are described as maliciously and treacherously allowing the malefactors to enter the city.

---

[1] Op. cit., p. 140.
[2] The bishop's predecessors had controlled the property there since the year 1100, and the girls in the houses, baring their breasts at the windows, became known as 'Winchester geese'.

70

A significant note found in these Inquisitions is that concerning Alderman Sibley who was criticised by some citizens for preparing to open the gates at London Bridge on the grounds that the rebels had just burned down the brothels round the corner. The alderman's reply is recorded as follows:–
> "What of it? That tenement has deserved destruction for the past twenty years!".[1]

Dobson states that recent researches have thrown grave doubts on the accuracy of the charges against these men, and it no longer seems possible to believe that a handful of aldermen could be responsible for admitting the rebels into London. On the other hand, in view of the definite allegation maintained against these men at the Inquisitions, it could be argued that they were in some way involved, for the simple reason that they had a genuine sympathy with the aims of the rebels. Like many business men, they were doubtless appalled by the corruption and inefficiency of the King and his ministers, and, like some of the gentry who supported the Rising, were prepared to throw their lot in with it, in the hope that it might produce better conditions for all. Alderman Sibley's remark, carefully recorded in the Rolls, and referred to above, "Quid ex hoc? Dignum est et dignum fuit everti per viginti annos elapsos!", certainly gives an indication that the motives of these aldermen were, to some extent, public spirited and morally based.

The combined rebel force moved westward through London. Froissart is clear who was leading it when he wrote:–
> "Then the captains, as John Ball, Jack Straw, and Wat Tyler, went throughout London and a twenty (thirty) thousand with them, and so came to the Savoy in the way to Westminster, which was a goodly house, by the Thames, and it pertained to the Duke of Lancaster".[2]

He goes on to say that the rebels sacked and destroyed this mansion, the town residence of the hated John of Gaunt, the King's uncle. This noble building, the finest in the city, was unrivalled in splendour and magnificence, for the Duke of Lancaster had made every effort to create in the Savoy, which

---

[1] CORAM REGE Roll – Easter 6 RICHARD II (KB27/488).
[2] Op. cit., p. 107.

he had inherited from his father-in-law, the very highest standard of luxury then known.

It is generally agreed that it was the Londoners who made the main attack on the Savoy, before the Kent or Essex men came up. But some of the latter undoubtedly joined in, though Wat Tyler had given strict instructions in the word of one report,

"Not one of you is to retain, for your own use, any object found there, under penalty of execution. For the whole community of the realm must know that we are not moved simply by avarice, but by a desire to establish what is just and right throughout our land."

One unfortunate Essex man, found concealing a silver plate under his smock, was immediately executed on Wat's orders. And a score or so, discovering wine casks in the cellars, became so drunk that they perished in the flames when the building collapsed, according to Knighton.

The *Anonimalle* report on the Savoy sacking is interesting, for its author writes:—

"And the commons of Kent received the blame for this arson, but some said the Londoners were really guilty of the deed, because of their hatred of the said Duke".[1]

On the whole, the country folk were fairly well behaved in their march through London. The *Anonimalle* continues:—

"At this same time the said commons took their way through London, doing no harm or injury, until they came to Fleet Street".[2]

Oman supports this by saying that the men of Kent and Essex behaved far better than might have been expected, and that it is recorded that many of them paid for their meals. He adds that they did no damage to private property that afternoon. He also quotes the visit of Alderman Horne to the Lord Mayor to assure him that the insurgents were honest folk and that he would wager his head that, if they were admitted within the walls, they would not do a pennyworth of damage.

But, as one of the prime objects of the rebels was to destroy

---

[1] Op. cit., pp. 140/150.
[2] Op. cit., pp. 140/150.

all evidence of their servitude, it was inevitable that they should turn their attention to the buildings where these records were stored. Consequently, after releasing the prisoners from the Fleet prison, they made a general assault on the Temple. They sacked the inns and dwellings of the lawyers, destroying an enormous quantity of charters, muniments and records. The lawyers and students had fled on seeing the commons arriving. One chronicler recorded it:–

"It was marvellous to see how even the most aged and infirm of them scrambled off, with the agility of rats or evil spirits".

Another building attacked was one of the official abodes of Sir Robert Hales, the Treasurer, much hated owing to the Poll Taxes he had introduced. This was the Priory of St. John's at Clerkenwell, headquarters of the Knights Hospitallers in England.

But on this first day, it was mainly public property which was destroyed, property and records of servitude. Many fine buildings were gutted. The *Anonimalle* reports:–

"Afterwards they came to the beautiful priory of the said hospital (St. John's) and set on fire several fine and pleasant buildings within it, a great and horrible piece of damage to the priory for all time to come. Then they returned to London to rest or to do more mischief".

The King, his mother and his ministers, with a bare six hundred armed men to protect them, awaited, with great anxiety in their hearts, to see what this mischief might be.

CHAPTER 16

The Mile End Meeting

THE royal party spent a restless night in the Tower. The flames from the burning Savoy Palace, and the St. John's Priory, must have been clearly seen by them all. With the King was his mother, his Chancellor, Archbishop Sudbury, his Treasurer, Sir Robert Hales, the Earls of Salisbury, Warwick, Arundel and Oxford, Sir Robert Knolles, Sir Thomas Percy, the Bishop of London, William Courtney, and the Lord Mayor, William' Walworth, among others.

Opinion was divided as to how to deal with this parlous situation. The Lord Mayor was for sallying out and attacking these "drunken ruffians", but the Earl of Salisbury, the most experienced soldier present, advised against this, and urged that negotiations should be tried. "If we begin what we cannot carry through, we should never be able to repair matters. It will be all over with us and our heirs, and England will be a desert", he is reported to have said, according to Froissart.

The first attempt to open up negotiations failed. The King sent a message asking the rebels to state their grievances in writing and then go home. The rebels replied that "all this was trifles and mockery", and told the royal messengers to return and bring back some better proposition.

After further consultation in the Tower with his advisers, Richard made an offer that he would meet the insurgents on the following morning in the meadows of Mile End, a favourite suburban rendezvous for the citizens of London, where he would consider their demands. The decision to do this had caused him no little anxiety. The Earl of Salisbury had convinced him that he should grant the rebels their demands and issue charters of freedom, which could easily be revoked later, and, in any case, had no validity until ratified by Parliament. This would doubtless be enough to persuade the gullible peasants to disperse and go home. They could then be dealt with piecemeal.

Richard II was fifteen years old at the time. A somewhat weak young man, unprepared to meet the situation which now confronted him, he was without the help of his three uncles. John of Gaunt was away on a mission in Edinburgh, Thomas of Woodstock was somewhere in the Welsh Marches, and Edmund of Cambridge had just sailed for Portugal. So Richard acquiesced. He would go and meet the rebels.

Early the following morning, June 14th, the King and his cortège rode out of the Tower followed by all his Council, with the exception of his Chancellor, his Treasurer and other officials – all hated by the people. The *Anonimalle* and Knighton say that he left these behind in order that they might have a chance of escaping when the rebel force was at Mile End. But Walsingham suggests that he left them behind as scapegoats to appease the popular wrath.

At the Mile End conference, Richard agreed to all the rebels' preliminary demands put forward by Tyler and Ball – freedom from serfdom, cheap land to be rented at four pence an acre, freedom to trade, and common justice for all. As a sign of the honesty of his intentions, he ordered thirty clerks to draw up charters bestowing freedom and amnesty on all. The rebel leaders must have been surprised that Richard gave in so easily. It is not recorded if they realised that charters given by the King were valueless until they had been ratified by Parliament. But, to most of the insurgents, especially the Essex men, the charters indicated that they had, indeed, gained all that they wanted.

But, a second question was brought up before Richard, the punishment of the ministers whom the rebels regarded as traitors. This is an important point, as many standard English history books refer to what subsequently happened in the Tower of London as a brutal murder. Contemporary accounts differ as to the terms granted by Richard in connection with the fate of traitors. The *Anonimalle Chronicle* reports as follows:–

"And Wat Teghler, their master and leader, prayed on behalf of the commons that the King would suffer them to take and deal with all the traitors against him and the law. The King granted that they should freely seize all who were traitors and could be proved to be such by process of law . . . And that they could go through all the realm of England and catch all traitors and bring them to him in safety, and then he would deal with them as the law demanded."[1]

The official city record of this grant is more definite. It reads,

"Whereupon our Lord the King granted that they might take those who were traitors against him and put them to death, wheresoever they might be found.".[2]

Kriehn says that he prefers to follow the city record, considering the fact that the King was entirely at the mercy of the insurgents, who would not have been satisfied thus to leave the matter to their chief enemies, the lawyers. This was certainly the understanding of the insurgents (who by virtue of this grant, straightaway proceeded to the Tower to kill the Chancellor and his companions), as well as that of the garrison, who admitted them.

Hilton and Fagan support this view, stating categorically that the occupants of the Tower were not murdered but executed as traitors by the King's authority on Tower Hill.[3]

On receiving this permission from the King, a force of four hundred men was despatched to the Tower to deal with the traitors. It is not clear who led this group. Wat Tyler and Thomas Farringdon are recorded as being at the head of the band. Froissart suggests that Ball, Tyler and Straw were all present in the Tower on this occasion, but it is unlikely that important leaders such as these latter would leave their main force at Mile End at this critical juncture. It is possible, therefore, that Farringdon alone would have led this group, especially as he was a Londoner with a personal grievance against Sir Robert Hales.

---

[1] Op. cit.,
[2] Letter Books of The City of London, (H.fol. 133 Latin), quoted in Riley's *Memorials of London*, p. 449.
[3] Op. cit., p. 283.

Farringdon and his men were not long in getting to the Tower. They found the drawbridge down and the guards lounging about. These made no effort to repel them, which indicates that some of the King's men were not entirely unsympathetic to the insurgents! The Archbishop had just finished saying Mass, and he come out of the chapel to greet them. "Here am I, your Archbishop", he said quietly. "I am no traitor". They pulled him outside, together with Sir Robert Hales, the Treasurer, John Legge, the Sergeant-at-Arms, and Brother William Appleton, physician and confessor to the King, all of whom were looked upon as traitors to the people.

The rebels set up a block on Tower Hill and proceeded with the execution; an Essex man from Colchester, John Starling, was appointed as executioner. The Archbishop was first. He died with great dignity, and Starling, being nervous, was forced to make several blows in order to complete his task. Hales had to be dragged to the place of execution, screaming and begging for mercy. Legge was carried to the block almost unconscious with fear. Brother William Appleton was the most composed of them all, saying his prayers calmly, and commending his soul to God.

Thus perished some of those whom the rebels looked upon as chief enemies. Sir Robert Hales was hated for his introduction of penal taxes, John Legge for his dishonest 'farming' of them, and, with his Commissioners, indecently assaulting young girls. Knighton reports his activities thus:—

"Therefore a certain John Leg with three colleagues asked the King to give him a commission to investigate the collectors of this tax in Kent, Norfolk and other parts of the country. They contracted to give the lord King a large sum of money for his assent; and most unfortunately for the King his council agreed. One of these commissioners came to a certain village to investigate the said tax and called together the men and women. He then, horrible to relate, shamelessly lifted the young girls to test whether they had enjoyed intercourse with men. In this way he compelled the friends and parents of these girls to pay the tax for them: many would rather pay for their daughters than see them touched in such a disgraceful way. These and similar actions by the said inquisitors much provoked the people".[1]

William Appleton, a Franciscan friar, had not only a great influence over King Richard, but was also a physician and chief political adviser to his hated uncle, John of Gaunt. He was, therefore, considered to be responsible for much of the Duke of Lancaster's repressive policy against the people.

In addition to these named, there were three other minor officials killed. It was perhaps, a small number of specific traitors to be executed in such a large revolt. But the rebels were not indiscriminate butchers, filled with a blood lust against everyone in authority. They knew who were the main enemies and were determined to eliminate them in the interests of the common good.

But it was sad that Archbishop Sudbury had to be included in the killing. He was a pious, well-meaning man who became a scapegoat for the whole set-up of unrighteous French wars and grinding taxation which was the main cause of the outbreak. He did accept the Chancellorship in January 1380, and, for this reason, he was inevitably involved.

Knighton bewails the involvement of the innocent with the guilty in this sad affair when he writes:—

"And so, alas and for sorrow! the two morning stars of the kingdom, the worthy with the unworthy and seven in all, were executed on Tower Hill before the King returned. For, as has been said, John Leg and his three colleagues were responsible for this irreparable loss".[2]

Later, a tribunal was set up, presided over by Thomas Farringdon and Alderman John Horne, to punish further enemies of the people. Another prominent person executed was Richard Lyons, a dishonest financier who had been impeached by the "Good Parliament" five years previously. Wat Tyler had served overseas under Lyons when the latter was one of the Sergeant-at-Arms of Edward III, and had been beaten by him for some dereliction of duty. He never forgave Lyons, and Froissart points out how he obtained his revenge by executing

---

[1] Op. cit., II, p. 129.
[2] Op. cit., II, pp. 132/3.

his former master.

After these executions, during the same day, there were many assaults on foreigners, and a number of Flemings and Lombards were killed. Jealousy over their successful business dealings was one of the obvious motives. And, in addition, certain lawyers, jurymen, persons connected with the levying of taxes, or known adherents to the Duke of Lancaster, became victims. It was a time for paying off old scores, in which the Londoners joined in eagerly, for there had been a longstanding feud between them and the Fleming community.

After the giving out of the charters, King Richard and his retinue returned to the Great Wardrobe near St. Paul's, where his mother had fled for shelter after the invasion of the Tower. Hearing what had happened in the Tower, Richard and his party decided to keep away from that ill-fated building. They moved into the unfortified Wardrobe, with strong hopes that their diplomacy at Mile End had succeeded.

But, the success of the Mile End plan was only partial. Now that they had received their charters, the peasants began to go home. Most of the Essex men trickled back, but Wat Tyler, John Ball and Jack Straw were left with the hard core of about twenty thousand men of Kent who remained. Like their leaders, they were feeling a bit dubious about the validity of those charters. They knew that Richard was a weak young man, dominated by his ministers. They were beginning to feel that there must be a trick somewhere. He had given in too easily.

CHAPTER 17

Revolt Spreads Far and Wide

AS Wat, John and Jack waited, doubtfully, with the twenty thousand determined Kentish men in the Mile End meadows, news started coming of the spread of the Revolt in the neighbouring counties. In Suffolk, a country priest had emerged as leader in the person of John Wrawe, rector of Ringsfield, near Beccles. He was a poor, discontented and ambitious man. Not a particularly good organiser, he possessed a loud and ready tongue, and this brought him forward into a position of leadership. Walsingham in *Chronicon Angliae* states that Wrawe had been in touch with Wat Tyler in London, and two messengers of the Great Society, Adam Worth and Thomas Sweyne of Coggeshall, had visited him early in June on their way from Essex to stir up Suffolk.

On June 12th, Wrawe gave the signal for revolt at Liston, on the Essex/Suffolk border, by sacking the manor of Richard Lyons, the financier. Then, after pillaging the estate at Overhall of Sir John Cavendish, Chief Justice of the King's Bench, hated for his enforcement of the Statute of Labourers, Wrawe marched on Bury St. Edmunds. On the evening of June 13th, he entered the town and was welcomed with open glee by the inhabitants who had been suffering from oppression from the Prior, John Cambridge. The latter fled but was eventually captured in a wood near Newmarket. Also captured was Sir John Cavendish who had a town house in Bury. He was endeavouring to cross the river at Brandon when a certain Katherine Gamon pushed off the boat into mid-stream, so that he was apprehended at the water's edge. Both men were beheaded, the mob parading their heads side by side on lances, sometimes placing the Judge's mouth to the Prior's ear, as if he were making his confession, and sometimes pressing the dead lips together for a kiss.

Wrawe remained in Bury St. Edmunds for the greater part of his short day of power. A strange facet in his character is revealed in the *Chronicon Angliae* report that, when his enthusiastic followers hailed him as 'King of the Commons', he refused the title, saying that he already possessed one crown, that of ecclesiastical tonsure, and, therefore, would not take another. He advised his supporters to elect his lieutenant, Robert Westbroun, a wealthy local man.

Meanwhile, at Sudbury, another lieutenant and fellow cleric of Wrawe's – Geoffrey Parfeye, vicar of the Church of All Saints in that town, together with his chaplain, Thomas, and another priest, Adam Bray, performed a remarkable military feat. With fourteen determined men, including Thomas Monchensey, Squire of Edwardstone, grandson of the wealthiest man in England, they made a dramatic ride across country, and stormed the town of Thetford, extorting twenty marks from the Mayor and Corporation by the threat that if this sum were not paid, Wrawe would come and burn the place to the ground. Certainly an example of the 'church militant' in action.

Over in Norfolk, things were beginning to move also. Stimulated by what had happened in their border town of Thetford, the commons began to rise. Here a leader of some ability was found, a dyer from the village of Felmingham, near North Walsham, named Geoffrey Litster. He was a man of some ability and evinced a real understanding of the purposes of the Revolt. A person of principle and possessing a certain amount of idealism, he was already winning mass support, not only from the working people, but from many of his country gentry, one of whom, Sir Roger Bacon, of Baconsthorpe, became his principal lieutenant. A knight working under a dyer was certainly a unique phenomenon in this Rising.

In Cambridgeshire, the Revolt had already started on June 13th. The leaders here were John Hanchach of Shudy Camp and Geoffrey Cobbe of Gazeley. Hanchach owned property in five townships and Cobbe was also a man of considerable estate. It is not known why two such wealthy landowners in the county should put themselves at the head of the Rising. Whether they acted from principle or self interest has never been discovered, but their appearance at the head of the Cambridge rebels does indicate a factor in the revolt, found elsewhere, that there was never lacking men of education or ability to take on its leadership.

On June 14th, a manor belonging to the Knights of St. John, whose prior was the unfortunate Sir Robert Hales, was attaked, and the two rebel leaders combined in an assault on the manors of Steeple Morden and Gildon Morden, belonging to Thomas Haselden, controller of the household of John of Gaunt. Haselden himself was fortunately absent in Scotland in the service of the Duke, otherwise he might have come to an evil end.

The troubles began in Hertfordshire at St. Albans on June 14th. A long and venomous struggle between the townsfolk and the Abbot of the Abbey, Thomas de la Mare, a hard-headed and litigious prelate, had come to a head in the town. Led by William Grindcobbe, a monk, the local people had risen and were demanding charters of freedom from domination by this wealthy and powerful churchman. A deputation was sent to Wat Tyler in London, and arrived there just in time for the end of the conference at Mile End. Grindcobbe, who was with the deputation, had a long discussion with Tyler who promised them his aid, and gave them instructions as to how they should deal with the abbott. The *Chronicon Angliae* describes it this way:–

> "And so they persuade Walter, although he had not planned to leave London or to send any of his followers away from himself, to promise to arrive with 20,000 men to shave the beards of the abbot, prior and other monks (that is, to behead them) if it proved necessary, or if the villeins sent for him".[1]

Kent, of course, was already in the hands of the rebels, as they marched up from Canterbury. Able lieutenants had been left behind by Wat and John to continue the control of the

---

[1] Op. cit., p.218.

county. The names of these are given in Kentish documents as John Hales of Malling, Robert Cave of Dartford, Alan Threder, William Hawke and John Ferrour. That things were proceeding satisfactorily for the rebel cause is endorsed by the report given by Rodney Hilton, as follows:–

> "The Isle of Thanet . . . was felt to be the natural focus for mobilisation. The lead was taken by men in St. John's Parish, Margate, including the sacristan and the parish clerk. Claiming to have a commission from Wat Tyler and Jack Straw, they made a proclamation in the church, organised the mobilisation of 200 men to burn the coroners and tax collectors' records, forbade tenants to perform services or allow distraints to be taken, should attempts at enforcement be made, and made a financial levy for the maintenance of proceedings against all the lords of Thanet. Thanet was an ancient unit of settlement and, as such, could be expected to be the area of regional organisation".[1]

Further outbreaks were now taking place in regions as far from the main source of rebellion as Yorkshire and Somerset. In Yorkshire, the chroniclers report risings in York, Beverley and Scarborough. Bedford, Northampton and Leicester were also affected, the revolts here taking the definite form of a rising of the smaller citizens against the greater. Leicester, in particular, was in a state of panic owing to its castle being a stronghold of the hated John of Gaunt. The abbot refused to take in the Duke's chattels for safe storage for fear of the rebels, and the latter's wife suffered similar treatment, when the rebellion broke out, by being refused admission to his great castle at Pontefract, for the same reason, eventually finding refuge in his estate at Knaresborough.

It was at Bridgewater in Somerset that another priest became leader. The vicar of the parish, Nicholas Frampton, being involved in an old quarrel about an advowson, took the opportunity to join the rebels and attack the house of the Knights of St. John in the town. Frampton was in London when the rebels entered the city and, having seen how the Essex and

---

[1] Op. cit., pp. 299/301.

83

Kent rebels dealt with the headquarters of the Knights Hospitallers at Clerkenwell, thought he might do the same at their Bridgewater house. He and the Somerset rebels sacked the place, and tore up all the bonds representing debts.

By and large, these outbreaks in the north and west were slow to develop, as communications were not easy and the wave of revolt was inevitably travelling less quickly in the outlying districts, cut off from the main centre of insurrection. But the overall picture was still an encouraging one as the news trickled back to the leaders, Wat, John and Jack at Mile End.

CHAPTER 18

Plotting in the Great Wardrobe

IN the Great Wardrobe, in Carter Lane, close by St. Paul's, Richard and his ministers were again in anxious consultation. Their attempt at appeasement had not been entirely successful for there was still a sizeable force of well-armed, unsatisfied Kentish men encampted at Mile End who were refusing to go home. Something more drastic had to be tried by the occupants of the Wardrobe if they wished to save their skins. Among the ministers present were one or two seasoned soldiers who had seen service in the French wars. Men like the Earls of Salisbury and Warwick, and Sir Robert Knolles, were not easily subdued. They knew from experience that a small force, outnumbered by a large one, could yet win the day, by trickery and cunning. So, together they worked out a plan.

They remembered that, some twenty years earlier, in France, King Charles of Navarre, was faced with the revolt of the 'Jacquerie', led by a resolute leader, Guillaume Câle, similar, in some ways, to Wat Tyler. Charles intimated that he was prepared to grant the rebels all that they asked. At a subsequent meeting, he manoeuvred Câle into appearing alone before him and his advisers. Then they slew Câle, and the rebel force, left leaderless, simply disintegrated. Here, the veterans, Salisbury and Warwick, doubtless urged, is a plan that can work for us also.

Kriehn supports this view of what had taken place in the Wardrobe on the night of June 14th, when he refers to the case of Guillaume Câle as "an interesting parallel", and concerning the actions of King Charles the Bad, he adds:–

"Now the English had been allies of Charles in this war, and his action must have been known to members of the Council. When we recall the awful death of Edward II, and of Richard II himself, we can hardly expect that the Council would have been troubled with many scruples over removing an intractable rebel whose influence prevented the insurgents from dispersing".[1]

So, on the morning of June 15th, Richard sent a message to the rebels at Mile End, saying he would meet them later that day outside Aldersgate, in the open area of Smithfield, where the cattle market was held (and continued to be held to the second half of the nineteenth century). He said he would be prepared to discuss with them any further grievances that might be outstanding.

Then, a short while later, the royal party emerged from the safety of the Wardrobe and, journeying to Westminster Abbey, took part in a ceremony which was strangely significant in view of what happened soon after. It is reported that, as the King and his followers approached Charing Cross, the Abbot of Westminster, together with the canons and vicars of St. Stephen's Chapel, came out to meet him in procession, clothed in their copes and barefooted. In this manner, they escorted him to the Abbey, at the great door of which he kissed the jewelled cross carried by a monk. Then, followed by the others, Richard went into the shrine of King Edward where he prayed devoutly and tearfully, and then made offering to the relics of the saints. His retinue dutifully followed his example, the lords, knights and squires vying with one another in their pious devotions, each striving to outdo the other in the size of his offerings. Some even managed to follow their monarch's example by shedding quite a measure of tears.

Finally, Richard spoke with the Abbey anchorite, made his confession to him, and remained with him for some little while. Then having ordered a proclamation to be made about the forthcoming Smithfield meeting, he rode away solemnly with his ministers and retinue, all with devout expressions on their faces.

---

[1] Op. cit., pp. 476/477.

86

The *Anonimalle* and Froissart both describe this remarkable piece of religious observance in some detail. Most modern historians have explained it as a pious act in order to seek the help of God in view of the ordeal before them. Charles Oman writes about it thus:–

> "Fully conscious that they were very possibly going to their death, but yet resolved to try this last experiment, Richard and his followers made ready for the interview by riding down to Westminster and taking the Sacrament before the high altar . . . The King shut himself up for a space with an anchorite, confessed to him, and received absolution. His retinue pressed round the shrine of the Confessor in long and devout prayers. At last they rode off together toward Smithfield, a body of about 200 men in all, most of them in robes of peace, but with armour hidden under their long gowns".[1]

Somehow, their desire to take the Sacrament, and especially Richard's wish to receive absolution, hardly seems to match up with the fact that they were all armed. It was obviously not a peaceful mission they were expecting to be involved in, but one which would require some military preparation, hidden carefully under robes of peace.

Some modern historians, Hilton and Fagan, and Lindsay and Groves, in particular, in their accounts of this incident, emphasise the fact that although the royal party were robed for a peaceful mission, under their cloaks and tunics they all wore steel and carried arms. This was to be a last desperate bid, made by terrified men, to save the situation. Both these accounts support the view of Kriehn that here was a well-thought-out plot being put into action.

It would seem, therefore, that the evidence would back up the American historian's assessment of the behaviour of Richard and his ministers on this occasion. They had no intention of going to seek a peaceful solution with John Ball, Wat Tyler and their men. They were going to carry out a pre-arranged plan, which they hoped would be the solution of their problem.

---

[1] Op. cit., pp. 72/73.

Dobson, referring to the account given by the continuator of the *Eulogium Historiarum,* points out that the details found in this chronicle seem reasonably plausible and lend some slight weight to the theory, originally and most forcefully expressed by Kriehn, that what happened at Smithfield may have been the result of a plot previously concocted by Richard and his advisers. The *Eulogium* details state:–

> "But the King, who was seriously concerned, and the burgesses, fearing the spoilation of the city, took council with Sir Robert Knolles about the way by which he could eject the rebels".[1]

Another significant point about this meeting was the way it was arranged so that the two parties were so far apart that very little of what was actually going on could be seen by them all. Smithfield was a very large open space just outside the walls at Aldersgate. Its extent may be judged from the fact that every week on a Friday, the city's cattle market was held here, and annually, the great St. Bartholomew's Fair took place.

Wat, John, Jack and their men arrived first at the meeting place, and were drawn up in battle array on the west side. A short while later, the King and his party came through Aldersgate and placed themselves on the opposite side in front of the Abbey Church of St. Bartholomew. There was a considerable distance between them, and, as it was some time after Vespers, evening shadows were possibly beginning to fall across this great field.

Richard and his retinue waited calmly. They had contrived to get the rebel force safely outside the walls of London. And, as a back up to their plan, Sir Robert Knolles and several others were now busy inside the city, rallying the trained bands and the retainers of the wealthy city merchants. A surprise force would undoubtedly be needed, in any eventuality.

---

[1] Op. cit., III, p. 353.

CHAPTER 19

Murder at Smithfield

IT is doubtful if any event in English history has been described in so distorted a fashion as that which took place at Smithfield on the late afternoon of Saturday, June 15th, 1381. History book after history book throughout the centuries has eulogised the brave conduct of a young boy king. The contemporary chroniclers started the paean of monarchial praise. We find Walsingham referring to the King showing marvellous presence of mind and courage for so young a man, and Froissart reporting that he performed a great bravery.

It all began when King Richard sent Mayor Walworth over to the other side of the Smithfield meadow to summon Wat Tyler to his presence to learn what new demands the rebels were now making. Tyler rode out to meet the King, on a small horse, accompanied by a single mounted companion bearing his banner. Accounts seem to have varied in detail as to what happened next, though there would appear to be a general similarity.

The following is largely the traditional idea of the Smithfield events and given in the picturesque account of English historian, J. R. Green:–

> "Many of the Kentishmen dispersed at the news of the King's pledge to the men of Essex, but a body of thirty thousand still surrounded Wat Tyler when Richard, on the morning of the fifteenth, encountered that leader by mere chance at Smithfield. Hot words passed between his train and the peasant chieftain who advanced to confer with the King, and a threat from Tyler brought on a brief struggle in which the Mayor of London, William Walworth, struck him with his dagger to the ground. 'Kill!

Kill!', shouted the crowd, 'they have slain our captain'. But Richard faced the Kentishmen with the same cool courage with which he faced the men of Essex. 'What need ye, my masters!' cried the boy King as he rode boldly up to the front of the bowmen. 'I am your captain and your King, follow me!'. The hopes of the peasants centred on the young sovereign; one aim of the their rising had been to free him from the evil counsellors who, they believed, abused his youth, and, at his words, they followed him with touching loyalty and trust until he entered the Tower. His mother welcomed him within its walls with tears of joy. 'Rejoice and praise God!', Richard answered, 'for I have recovered today my heritage which was lost, and the realm of England!'."[1]

Actually, things happened quite differently. The meeting was not accidental, but pre-arranged. When Tyler reached the King's party, he dismounted and, kneeling before Richard, assured him of the loyalty of the Commons. Wat presented his further demands, embodying safeguards against the Statute of Labourers, free hunting and fishing, and a drastic reformation of the Church. Richard agreed with all these, promising to include them in the charters. Tyler then asked for a drink with which to refresh himself and, mounting his horse, prepared to return to his men. In the meantime, the King's followers had gathered round him in such a way that he was not able to be seen by his own men across the field. Then, one of the King's party, a young Kentish nobleman, repeatedly insulted Tyler, hoping that it would provoke him into some action which would necessitate his arrest.

Tyler, exasperated beyond measure, drew his own dagger in anger, and hit out at the Lord Mayor who was approaching him in a menacing fashion, the blow merely glancing off the latter's cuirasse. This gave the King's supporters the excuse to attack Wat, Mayor Walworth striking the first blow, which sheared through the rebel leader's shoulder. The Kent squire, Ralph Standish, then ran him through the body. Reeling from this combined attack, Wat broke through the circle of his enemies,

---

[1] Op. cit., pp. 478/479.

shouting, "Treason! Avenge me, ye commons!", rode twenty yards towards his followers, before falling from his horse, mortally wounded.

What followed next was the most critical moment in the whole rebellion, for it would appear probable that Richard and his followers would be massacred. It seems inconceivable that the rebels would have stood by idly while their leader was slain, and take no immediate action. The answer to this is found in the evidence of the chroniclers themselves, the *Anonimalle*, the *Evesham* and the *Eulogium*. These fairly reliable sources all state that the rebels did not know what was going on at the time. The *Anonimalle* writes that "they did not know for certain how it happened"; the *Evesham* monk implies that the people did not know of Tyler's fate when he tells us that immediately afterwards they demanded to know where their leader was. The Continuator of the *Eulogium* gives the most direct testimony when he affirms that, during the struggle, the people asked what the King was doing with their advocate, and were informed that he was being made a knight. They were further led to believe that he would rejoin them in St. John's Field. Froissart adds support to this when he reports that "they environed him (Tyler) all about, whereby he was not seen of his company".

Chroniclers are agreed that some sort of rudeness or audacity by Tyler, in rinsing his mouth and spitting out the contents in front of the King, did cause some resentment on the part of the latter's followers. But this was but the action of an over-confident man, stimulated by the thought that victory was now within his grasp, and was certainly no reason for his assassination.

The much reported action of King Richard, in spurring over to the rebels and offering to be their leader, gave occasion for the fine speeches recorded in the Chronicles. But this was the final act in the drama that had previously been worked out. The rebels had been already told that the King had made Tyler a knight, that he would meet them in St. John's Field, and that the King had granted their demands. So, they followed him, convinced that their cause had been won, and that a great revolution had been accomplished.

To make finally sure of the complete subjection of the rebels, Mayor Walworth had ridden back into the city to summon the loyal forces that Sir Robert Knolles had been assembling, which, emerging from the city gates, surrounded the now confused insurgent army. The arrival of the King's forces at St. John's Field within half an hour indicated that the whole thing was obviously planned. It was all over so quickly. Careful planning and good staff work had won the day for the King.

It is amazing how similar the plan was to that, previously referred to, which was carried out against Guillaume Câle in the French 'Jacquerie" revolt. In this case, a French chronicler reported that when Câle was surrounded and killed, his supporters "knew not for certain how it was". The ruling classes of England and France were always very close together, bound by ties of relationship and business interests, and obviously knew how to share their tricks.

Kriehn, who has made a detailed analysis of these Smithfield events, gives a clear summary.

"Was the death of Tyler an accident on the part of the King's followers, the deserved result of his insolence, or was it a preconceived deed, part of a successful plan to effect the dispersal of the insurgents? Let us examine the meagre evidence.

"(1) The meeting at Smithfield was so arranged that the multitude did not see what was going on. The King did not ride over to the commons as at Mile End, where they could see him, but stayed on the side of the field nearest London, the gates of which were held by his partisans. Tyler was conducted to the far side of the field, out of reach and sight of his men.

"(2) He was deliberately provoked into an action which would give a pretext for attacking him. After he desired to return, the Kentish valet, with the King's permission, deliberately and repeatedly offered him the greatest insult imaginable. The lords ordered the young nobleman to go before him "pur veier que il (i.e. Tyler) voideroit faire deuant le roy"[1] i.e. to see if he would not

---

[1] 'Anonimalle Chronicle, p. 519.

commit some act in the King's presence which would give a pretext for arresting or slaying him.

"(3) Everybody on the King's side was in readiness for the results of Tyler's death. Only half-an-hour elapsed from the time when the Mayor left the King until the army of rescue appeared at St. John's Field. It would not have been possible to raise the men of the twenty-four different wards of London, issue in strategic order from the different gates, and surround the rebels in so brief a time, unless these forces had been waiting in readiness. That the lords' retinues and men-at-arms were in readiness is repeatedly stated by Froissart. Furthermore, the Mayor had secured control of the city gates, which up to this time had been opened at the will of the insurgents. Both he and the aldermen wore cuirasses concealed under their robes, else Wat's dagger-thrust would have had quite different results. In this light, the religious preparations of the King and his train at Westminster acquire a new significance; we can understand why so dangerous an attempt should be thus solemnly ushered in. The details of the plot must have comprised what actually occurred. The King consented to Tyler's radical demands, but with no intention of fulfilling them, in order to get the people away from the city and to placate them, in view of the intended violence to Tyler. That his death rather than his capture was planned, is rendered likely by the Mayor's action in beheading him".[1]

After Wat Tyler had fallen wounded from his horse, his followers carried him into the hospital of St. Bartholomew's Abbey. Mayor Walworth had then sought him out, and had him dragged to the square, where, unconscious or already dead, he was decapitated, and his head carried before the commons on a pole.

Kriehn sums up the whole issue with the words:–

"The death of Tyler, however, was no accident, but a state murder, the chief part of a successful scheme to effect the dispersal of the insurgents. The plot was hatched in the

---

[1] Op. cit., pp. 475/476.

King's Council, and was daringly carried out by London's intrepid Mayor and England's youthful King ... The most likely explanation of Tyler's death is that it was one of the state murders that darken English history".[1]

Thus ended the first ever mass rising of the English people for freedom and justice, an occurrence concerning which history has not yet made up its mind.

[1] Op. cit., pp. 463/477.

CHAPTER 20

Colchester Happenings

ALTHOUGH the Revolt was over, as far as London was concerned, there was still considerable activity elsewhere. While the Kentish men were being herded back over London Bridge to their homes, half cowed, half tricked and sullen, the Essex rebels, who had dispersed with their charters, were now beginning to doubt if these hard won documents were worth the parchment on which they were engrossed. Immediately after the Smithfield debacle, John Ball, with other Essex leaders such as Adam Michel, John Kyrkeby and Henry Baker, fell back, with a contingent of local men who had remained with them, to the thickly wooded country to the north-east of London. Here they were joined by large numbers of dissatisfied Essex men, and began to regroup and re-organise in order to continue the struggle.

While they were doing this, the people of Colchester itself were playing out their own individual part in the drama. Hitherto it has been assumed that it would not be possible to obtain much information about Colchester happenings in 1381, as the vital Rolls, covering this year, are missing. But, now that we have been able to examine the printed Volume IV of the Benham transcription, some important evidence of active Colchester participation can now be revealed for the first time.

It is strange that Benham, in his introduction to Volume III of the Court Rolls (1372–1379) should state that none of the Colchester Rolls were destroyed in the Peasants' Rising of 1380–1381, but that Morant may have lost a number of them during his researches in the eighteenth century. Further, Benham adds that the years between 1372 and 1379 were not specially eventful in English history. He does admit that the insurrectionary spirit was no doubt smouldering, but there is nothing to indicate this in the Colchester Rolls which, he remarks, as usual contain no references to national events. This was published in 1941, and Benham died in 1944, leaving behind the unpublished but printed (alas, not indexed!), Volume IV.

This Volume IV was apparently in the course of preparation when Benham died and the war ended. That it was never actually published was doubtless due to this combination of circumstances. If Benham had lived he would, without doubt, have made references to these important records of Colchester events in an introduction to this later volume and, possibly, would have corrected his previous statement. The ending of the war also contributed to lack of interest in the publication of Volume IV. There were known to be several salvage drives carried out by Colchester Borough Council in the immediate post-war period, when much that was considered to be dry, antiquated stuff was destroyed. We are lucky to have the half-dozen or so copies of Volume IV, one of which came into the author's hands in 1975, and others are now in the Castle and Borough Reference Libraries.

This evidence in Volume IV of the Rolls, which commences in September 1381, the previous year – alas – being missing!, reveals that on June 16th 1381, (the day after Wat Tyler was killed at Smithfield), an attack was made on the Town Hall, and Court Rolls and Muniments taken away and burned. This attack was led by a certain William-atte-Appelton, supported by John Waltham and John Tasseler (*Court Rolls* dated Oct. 4th, 1381, Vol. IV, pp. 52/56).

Another attack is recorded on September 30th 1381, when St. John's Abbey was stormed, on a date unspecified, and Rolls and Muniments again destroyed. Among those taking part were John Forde of Brightlingseye, Willam Pash, Henry Heukyn and John Broke (Vol. IV, p. 52).

The following are the records in detail:–

LAWHUNDRED
Monday after Feast of St Michaelmas (Sept. 30th 1381)
(RIOTERS)

PRESENTMENTS

John Forde, of Brightlingseye, Wm. Pach, Henry Heukyn, John Broke, by force and violence entered the Abbey of St. John's, and carried off the Rolls and Muniments of that Abbey. (p.52)

PLEAS

Friday after St. Michael's Day (Oct. 4th 1381)

(ANOTHER ECHO OF THE REBELLION)

Wm-atte-Appelton was charged with having, on Sunday, June 16th, 4Richd II (1381), together with others, entered the Hall of the Commonalty and the Treasury of the same, and threatened to burn the Rolls and Muniments which were in the Treasury, whereby they were removed, so that for five weeks next following the Courts were suspended. He denied the charge, and was ready to prove, etc. (p.52)

(OTHER REBELS?)

John Waltham and John Tasseler with Wm-atte-Appelton summoned by the Bailiffs. Enquiry ordered. (p.53)

Wednesday after Feast of St. Luke (Oct. 23rd 1381)

(RIOTER SENT TO PRISON – COURT ROLLS TAKEN AWAY: RELEASE OF RIOTER ON PAYMENT OF 6s 8d)

Enquiry between the Bailiffs and Wm-atte-Appelton by oath of Robt-atte-Ford and a jury, find William guilty of entering with force and arms the Hall of the Commonalty and Treasury of the same and carrying off Court Rolls and Muniments of the said town, so that the Courts of the town ceased for five weeks : it is ordered that he be put in prison, in charge of the Sergeant, until, etc.

The said William pays a fine of half a mark (6s 8d) for his release from prison, by pledge of Thomas Gogger and John Bishop. (p.56)

These are the only records, in the existing Rolls, of Colchester men actually attacking buildings and destroying Rolls. They are, therefore, very important ones.[1] The attack on the Town Hall, coming as it did on the day after the death of the rebel leader in London, may have been due to the news of this reaching Colchester and acting as a stimulus to some of the town's inhabitants to destroy all evidence while they could. As Colchester was in rebel hands from early on in the Revolt, it can be assumed that the leaders in the town had kept closely in touch with the London events. Being but fifty-six miles from the capital, messengers on fast horses could easily have reached them late in the night of the 15th of June, or early the following morning, with the dreadful news of the Smithfield humiliation. Being astute men, they would, in all possibility, have determined to get rid of any records detrimental to themselves before it was too late. It does seem strange that they should have left it so long before doing this, but the absence of the previous Rolls, for Michaelmas 1380–1381, means that we are unable to find out what exactly went on in Colchester during this vital period.

But from what we have found recently, there was obviously something taking place there, in spite of the late Mr Benham's complacent assumption to the contrary. Writing in the Preface to the Colchester *Oath Book and Red Parchment Book* which he translated and transcribed in 1907, he states:–

> "But although the official records are reticent as to the more important incidents in national history, we can recognise the fact that Colchester was often, if not always, in sympathy with revolution. *One may even suspect some slight indication of friendly interest in Wat Tyler's rebellion*".[2]

In view of what is now known about Colchester in the early

---

[1] Confirmation of this is found in the Leger Book of St. John's Abbey, Colchester, as follows:– "Indenture by which the monks of St. John's leave to Roger Kyrkeston, burgess of Colchester, tenements in West Donyland (Rowhedge) at the will of the lord, as appears more fully in the first court of Donyland and Greenstead, *post rumorem et combustionem rotulorum,* (after the disturbance and the burning of the rolls), held 20 December 1381." [See *The Leger Book of St. John's Abbey, Colchester,* by J. L. Fisher – Transactions, Essex Archaeological Society, N.S. XXIV (1944–49), p. 113]

[2] italics mine.

days of June 1381, and of John Ball's activities there, this statement must surely be classified as the historical understatement of all time!

CHAPTER 21

Essex and Kent Men Involved

AS it was the Essex and Kent men who were the main actors in the London drama, it is to be expected that we should find some reference to them by name in the various accounts of the Revolt. In the contemporary chronicles, in the Red Paper Book, the Oath Book, and the Court Rolls of the Borough of Colchester, mention is made of the activities of prominent rebels from the two counties.

The chronicles, of course, give prominence to the well-known leaders such as John Ball, Wat Tyler and Jack Straw, who feature all the way through. Additional Essex names of rebels are listed – John Awedyn, Thomas Baker of Fobbing, John Hermare and Nicholas Gromond of Havering-atte-Bower, John Kyrkeby of Colchester, and John Starling. Kent men referred to are Robert Cave of Dartford, John Hales of Malling, Abel Ker from Erith, Ralph Rugge, Thomas Scot, Alan Threder, William Hawke and John Ferrour.

In the Colchester Court Rolls, some rebel names have appeared before the Revolt, as troublemakers, being indicted for offences such as trespass, assault and debt. John Kyrkeby, ex-burgess of the town, was always in trouble, over money matters, before he came to London with the rebels. Although one report indicates that he was killed in a London street battle, Walsingham states that he was executed in London together with Jack Straw and Alan Threder. But his name appears in the Colchester Rolls on January 28th, 1382, and several times in 1383, still coping with his eternal problem of debts!

Adam Michel, a prominent Colchester rebel, was also a

Burgess, and actually held the important position of Sergeant of the South Ward. He was constantly before the Court for various offences, and during the Revolt, he incited the townsfolk to slaughter Flemings, several of whom were killed. He appears to have survived the Revolt, being charged on December 30th 1381, with incitement to assault. His wife, Joan, a woman brewster, was continually arraigned for brewing without paying tax, and on January 19th, 1388, she was summonsed because she 'opstupat garderobam', (stops up a privy), till it rains, when a great stench goes out opposite Thomas Frauncey's dwelling."

Henry Baker, the Manningtree Bailiff and chief recruiter for the Colchester insurgents, appears again, after the Revolt, on a charge of non payment of rent for a piece of land.

It is noticeable that these three latter are men of some standing – a burgess, a sergeant, and a bailiff. This would give support to the view that this revolt was more than one by mere peasants and serfs. That reasonably prosperous citizens were prepared to join in, must indicate that the genuine dissatisfaction with the way the country was being run was widely felt. To join the rebels seemed to some to provide a real chance to get wrongs righted. Of this, Powell writes:–

"From the lists of names which occur on the *Coram Rege* Rolls and elsewhere, it would seem that a fair proportion of the tradesmen and citizen class from the towns had thrown in their lot with the insurgents".[1]

Of the Kent men, Abel Ker, of Erith, is known to have captained a band which captured the monastery of Lesness, and frightened the Abbot into swearing on oath to support them. Robert Cave, of Dartford, led an assault on Rochester, and John Hales, of Malling, headed the movement on Canterbury, attacking the castle and Town Hall and residences of high officials.

There is definite evidence as to the fate of some of the Kent and Essex rebels. According to chronicler Walsingham, Alan Threder and John Starling were executed, at the same time as Jack Straw, in London. Froissart records that Thomas Baker

---

[1] Op. cit., p. 62.

and William Gildbourne, both of Fobbing, were executed at St. Albans. Robert Cave was, apparently, imprisoned for some considerable period, the only man who seems to have endured a long stretch in gaol. He was not released until 1392, and, considering the known state of medieval prisons, it can be assumed that this baker of Kent must have possessed a very strong constitution.

The fate of the men who attacked Colchester Town hall on June 16th provides a strange sequel, according to the Court Rolls. William-atte-Appelton, a fuller, was apparently also a burgess, and, although sentenced to prison, he was soon released after payment of half a mark (6s 8d). He appears to have been a litigious person as his name is found in connection with disputes on a number of occasions in the Rolls. His fellow rebels, John Waltham and John Tasseler, a webber from Wivenhoe, near Colchester, subsequently both became burgesses, and the former was actually a juror of the Law Hundred at the time of the offence. There is no record as to how they were treated by the Court, but the Rolls indicated that they both became prosperous. Waltham was, in 1379, executor of the will of the rector of St. Mary's, Creeting, and inherited lands in Colchester from him. Shortly after the attack on the Town Hall, he was living with a woman named Agnes Herdes. John Tasseler later rented lands in the town, "lying in a certain lane extending from Northscherde as far as North Bridge".

That men of such substance could be described as 'rioters' and 'rebels' is rather remarkable, more so in that they appear to have got off almost scot free. This would confirm Rodney Hilton's assumption that the Rising was one in which people of all classes took part. He writes:—

"The names of the indicted, and of those whose property was confiscated, would naturally tend to include those men and women who took a prominent, if not always leading, part in the events. A full list of all participants might suggest a rather different balance between different occupations, but with the exception of the clergy, this difference might not have been all that great. The proportion of the well-to-do against those of middling or lesser fortune, and of craftsmen against agriculturalists, suggests that the social composition of the rebellious bands reflected the stratification of contemporary society. In other words, the rising was one of the whole people below the ranks of those who exercised lordship in the countryside and established authority in the towns".[1]

Then, there were the real 'lumpenproletariat', those who were often in trouble, in debt, cited as vagrants, and the like. There was a Walter Bowyer, frequently in the Rolls, who once charged Nicholas Bowyer, a relation, with assault and "drawing blood". Robert Swynesford, a long time bad hat and night vagrant, broke into the house of John White, the tiler, and was constantly cited for "trespass". Then there was a ne'er-do-well chaplain named John Isenmongre, who appears on many charges, one of which was "for being a night vagrant, standing under men's walls, and listening to their plans", (October 3rd, 1378), and another "for being a common handler of fish on the bank" (March 28th, 1379). He may have been one of the gang who once beat up John Ball in 1377 (See Chapter 4). It is remarkable to find that Isenmongre sued the same William Crabbe for entering his house and attempting to take away goods, at the same Court and at the same time as John Ball and John Proude were doing likewise. It looks as if they were all chaplains together in the same lodging house in East Street owned by the unfortunate Mr Crabbe.

· French historian, André Réville, who died at the early age of twenty-seven, was only able to complete the first part of his projected history of the great English Revolt of 1381. It contains many valuable and interesting transcripts of documents, among these a list of a number of Court indictments from the Colchester–Manningtree–Mistley area after the Revolt. Out of a total of seventeen rebels and one 'enemy of the people', all but three appear in the Colchester Rolls. They are: John Somenour, William Chaumeberlain, Robert Waleys, John Webbe, John Langham (or Longham), John Danewe, Geoffrey Paynman, John Glasene, John Thecchere, John Lucas, John Dawe, Adam Michel, Henry Baker, and the 'enemy' was Thomas Hardyng.

It would seem then that there is quite a large body of

---

[1] Op. cit., p. 184.

evidence of the involvement of Colchester men in the 1381 Rising, and of their activity in the London scene. We know that a number of them, some of the best ones, perhaps, lost their lives in this struggle for social justice. We find that there were some who managed to survive – astute and quick thinking ones, who lived on to fight another day. But the general picture is that of a concerned people playing their part in a great dramatic episode in the history of our nation.

CHAPTER 22

Suffolk, Norfolk, Cambridge and St. Albans

WHILE John Ball and the remnants of the Essex force were painfully licking their wounds and regrouping to the north-east of London, the Revolt was still developing elsewhere. The news of the death of Wat Tyler, their leader, was now beginning to circulate in the country areas and, although it was a devastating blow to the rebels, there was still quite a lot of fight left in them in the rural districts.

In the adjoining county of Suffolk, the western part was still under the control of the priest, John Wrawe. Among his chief supporters was Sir Thomas Cornerd, from the parish of Great Cornard, near Sudbury, a knight who according to the chronicles, had joined the revolution for discreditable reasons, as he appeared to spend most of his time plundering the estates of his neighbours. Wrawe, himself, led one or two excursions, sacking Mettingham Castle, near Bungay, on June 18th, and, on the following day, he held an assize in the town of Beccles, presiding over the execution of Geoffrey Southgate, an unpopular resident. On the same afternoon, he went on to sack the manor of Hugh Fastoff at Bradwell, carrying off goods to the value of over £400 from the owner, who had been one of the Commissioners for the collection of the Poll Tax.

On June 16th, Ipswich was entered by the insurgents. At their head was what had become by now the inevitable priest, John Battisford, the rector of Bucklesham. Together with co-leader, Thomas Sampson, of Harkstead, they sacked the houses of the Archdeacon of Suffolk, and John Cobat, another local Poll Tax collector. A further group of rebels spread themselves over the Eastern Hundreds of Suffolk, seeking a much hated Justice of the Peace named Edward Lakenheath. He was chased to the coast, but escapted in a boat, only to fall into the hands of a French privateer, who held him to ransom for the sum of 500 marks, a sum which, in view of the fact that his five manors had been devastated, he found difficulty in collecting after the Revolt.

In Western Norfolk, there was not so much activity, though on June 17th, two unpopular Justices, John Holkham and Edmund Gurney, the latter steward of the estates of John of Gaunt, were chased by a group of rebels led by a certain Walter Tyler, namesake of the leader killed two days earlier. These Justices were also pursued, for twenty-four hours, to the coast where they procured a small boat at Holme-by-the-Sea, and launched it out into the deep. Their pursuers followed them, in a larger boat, and, after an exciting twenty-mile chase, the two magistrates were about to be overtaken when night came down and hid them from their enemies. Holkham and Gurney slipped away, landed at Burnham, and escaped.

In Eastern Norfolk, there was much greater activity as Geoffrey Litster was now getting organised. Declaring himself an enemy of both the traitors who were conducting the King's government and the oppressive landlords who were enforcing manorial customs, he soon gained massive support. On June 17th, he collected his forces on the traditional mustering ground of Mousehold Heath, a mile or so distant from the city of Norwich. In addition to Sir Roger Bacon, he had persuaded a number of other country knights to join his forces, Sir William Morley, Sir John Brewes, Sir Stephen Hales and Sir Roger Scales. Whether these joined voluntarily, or were frightened into supporting the rebel force is not known, but it is recorded that another knight, Sir Robert Sale, a veteran of the French wars under Edward III, had his doubts and was killed in an argument that ensued.

Litster and his huge army moved on Norwich where the gates were closed, but these were soon opened to welcome him. Apparently, the Mayor, Aldermen and some of the wealthy citizens were in favour or resisting the insurgents, but the ordinary people of the town were desirous of admitting them, and their will prevailed. Litster entered Norwich in triumph, his troops being led by Sir Roger Bacon in full armour, with pennons flying and in warlike array. He was soon established in the area, and sent a force under Sir Roger to take Yarmouth, which he did on June 18th.

Litster now styled himself 'King of the Commons', and named his host 'The Great Company'. Like Tyler, he maintained good disicpline, and it is interesting to note that, after the suppression of the rebellion, there were comparatively few indictments for theft and robbery from the area under his control. His main concern was the destruction of deeds and Court Rolls, and the orderly arrangement of land possession.

On June 20th, having heard about the death of Wat Tyler, Litster sent an embassy to London to request the grant of a charter of manumission for all Norfolk, such as had been given to the men of Essex and Kent at Mile End, also asking for a general pardon for himself and his followers for all irregularities committed during the past week. His ambassadors were the two knights, Sir William Morley and Sir John Brewes. With them he added three of his most trusted lieutenants, who bore the peculiar names of Trunch, Skeet and Kybytt. What happened to his somewhat ill-assorted group, we shall hear later.

In Cambridgeshire, on Saturday, June 15th, the very day of the Smithfield murder, rebellion flared up at at least a dozen separate points in the county. That evening, the town of Cambridge, where friction between the townsfolk and the University had been developing for some time, rose, the signal for insurrection being the tolling of the bells of Great St. Mary Church. Corpus Christi College, which owned much property in the town, and which was founded by John of Gaunt, was sacked without resistance. University archives from St. Mary's Church and the library in the House of the Carmelites (now Queen's College), were soon destroyed. A bonfire was made in the Market Square, and a certain old woman named Margery Starre is recorded as having taken part in the destruction of documents by leaping about and crying, "Away with the learning of the Clerks! Away with it!", as she consigned parchment after parchment to the flames. After this, the townsfolk prepared a document by which the University was made to surrender all the privileges which it had enjoyed under royal donations.

The Priory of Barnwell was then attacked by a force of over one thousand townsfolk, led by the Mayor of Cambridge, Edmund Redmeadow, a feeble and cautious man, who subsequently claimed that he had been forced to take the lead by threat of beheading if he did not comply. Walls were pulled down, trees felled, fish-ponds drained and turves carried off to store for the winter. The Prior was compelled to sign a bond of £2,000 guaranteeing that he would not prosecute any individual for damage done at that monastery.

In Hertfordshire, the main struggle still centred round the town of St. Albans, and the strife between the townsfolk and the Abbot of the Abbey had now come to a head. Fortified by Wat Tyler's promise, the citizens took matters into their own hands and proceeded to put an end to the authority of the hated prelate. His fishponds were drained, his hedges broken down, his game killed, and his land cut up and divided into plots for the citizens. The peoples' millstones, which a previous Abbot had stolen, in order to prevent them from milling their own corn and which were paving the monastery floor, were pulled up and returned to their rightful owners. Negotiations were going on with the Abbot in order to obtain from him a charter emancipating the inhabitants.

But, on Sunday morning, June 16th, the news from Smithfield was known in the town, and the citizens became more cautious and drew up a new moderate charter for themselves. Deputations began to come in from the surrounding countryside, and, on June 19th, the Abbot was visited by turbulent groups from all the manors belonging to the Abbey. After violent harangues and threats, Abbot de la Mare was forced to ratify the King's general abolition of serfdom. He gave up his rights over his serfs, granted them free hunting, fishing and exemption from previous tolls and dues. This great victory was possibly due to the determined leadership of the monk, William Grindecobbe, one of the sincere and disinterested leaders who emerged during the Revolt.

Risings in Hertfordshire were not confined to the town of St. Albans. Similar activities were going on in towns like Tring, where a bonfire was made of manorial archives. Houses of two Justices of the Peace were attacked in Watford, and the Priors of Redbourne and Dunstable were forced to draw up charters emancipating their tenants. But, on the whole, things were much quieter in Hertfordshire than in neighbouring Essex. Only two murders were reported from the whole of the county. One of these, that of an unpopular bailiff at Cublecote, was committed by a group headed by Hugh, the parson of Puttenham. The clergy, indeed, appeared to be involved in every county, but there were, inevitably, bad hats among them, and the proportion of these was certainly no higher than that in any other comparable body of men.

So, undeterred by the bad news from Smithfield, the country districts fought on. They knew that their cause was a just one, and new leaders were still arising, who, they felt, could lead them to the fulfillment of their hopes.

CHAPTER 23

King Richard Strikes Back

THE King and his ministers struck back hard. They had had the fright of their lives, and their determination to avenge themselves on those who had caused them such humiliating fear was almost in the nature of a reflex action. Never in their wildest dreams had they imagined that ignorant peasants could ever rise up and threaten their position of authority and privilege. That they had done so, had produced in the nobility a traumatic condition from which it would take them a long time to recover.

While the remnant of the Essex men were regrouping under John Ball and other leaders, north-east of London, Richard and his ministers decided to move against them at once. London had now been secured, and, with the rebels much demoralised by the death of their military leader, it was felt that now was the time to strike back. The King's army was augmented by a force commanded by his uncle, Thomas of Woodstock, Earl of Buckingham, who, hearing that the rebels had been defeated in London, had hurried back from the Welsh Marches in order to be in at the kill. On June 18th, the nobility, their confidence now restored, assembled their forces on the rebels' old camping ground at Blackheath, and prepared to move out into Essex, bent on revenge. On June 23rd, they were at Waltham, and made camp in the meadows, near the Abbey.

The rebel force was nearby in the forest area, and, hearing that Richard and his army had arrived at the town, they sent a deputation to the King asking for a ratification of the promises made at Mile End. The royal answer was short and to the point. Richard informed them that his pledges made during the Revolt counted for nothing, having been extorted under duress, and that, anyhow, they had no validity until they had been ratified by Parliament. He then added a threat which chronicler Walsingham records in detail in the following words:—

"Oh you wretched men, detestable on land and sea, you who seek equality with lords are not worthy to live! You would certainly have been punished by the most shameful death if we had not determined to observe the laws concerning envoys. But as you have come here in the guise of envoys, you will not die now but may keep your lives until you have accurately informed your fellows of our reply. So give this message to your colleagues from the King. 'Rustics you were, and rustics you are still; you will remain in bondage, not as before but incomparably harsher. For as long as we live, and by God's grace, rule over the Realm, we will strive with mind, strength and goods to suppress you so that the rigour of your servitude will be an example to posterity. Both now and in the future, people like yourselves will always have your misery as an example before their eyes; they will find you a subject for curses, and will fear to do the sort of things you have done'."[1]

Some modern authors have tried to prove that the young King Richard had a sentimental sympathy for the oppressed peasantry and that it was his evil counsellors who were forcing him to oppress them. They even quote the rumour that the King has sent secret messages of support to the rebels, sending them his banner under which some of them fought. It is true that the rebels did have a misplaced loyalty to their King, as it turned out to be. Their slogan 'With King Richard and the True Commons' was, perhaps, one of the saddest of misconceptions suffered by them, and would look like one of the best confidence tricks perpetrated on them. Richard's intemperate diatribe at Waltham certainly proves this point.

Reeling from this tirade of vindictive invective, the deputation reported back to Ball and his companions in the forest. They decided to move further into Essex, and, in the vain

---

[1] Op. cit., pp. 312–17.

hope of defending their newly won liberties by force of arms, they sent out a summons for a general mobilisation from the villages of Great Baddow and Rettendon, south of Chelmsford. Joined by these additional forces, they retreated to the small town of Billericay, about twenty miles from London. Here, they prepared to defend themselves against the oncoming royal army.

The so-called Battle of Billericay was one of two real clashes of arms between the rebels and the King's forces that took place during the whole of the rebellion. The Government and the insurrection had not previously had an opportunity of any trial of strength in the open field. But, when it did come, it was an occasion when the odds were stacked very much in favour of the attackers. For the King and his ministers had had ample time to gather an efficient and overwhelming force with which to face the rebel assembly. Walsingham describes its composition thus:

"On the death, already mentioned, of that most arrogant rascal, Walter Tylere, the hope and trust of the rustics collapsed. But, as the King and his counsellors were yet in doubt as to whether the people were still disposed to evil, they granted charters of manumission and pardon to them, as we have said, and allowed them to depart. After this, the King assembled an army of Londoners and sent messengers into the country asking all those who loved him and honoured the realm to hurry to him in London, well-armed and on horseback; no one was to come weaponless and no one on foot and those who lacked either arms or horses were to stay at home. And so it happened that within three days, 40,000 properly armed horsemen had gathered around the King. Each day the King himself went out to Blackheath to review the number of new arrivals, riding first among his armed men on a great war horse. His standard was carried before him and he enjoyed being seen in his army and recognised as their lord by his men".[1]

Allowing for this chronicler's obvious exaggeration of the

---

[1] Op. cit., pp. 312–17.

numbers of the royal force, it is clear that the 'rustics' as he calls them, would be hopelessly outnumbered when it came to a pitched battle. But, with the odds against them, fight they did.

The rebels took up their positions on the sloping meadows near Billericay with a large wood behind them. They stockaded themselves with rows of stakes in the front, and protected their flanks with ditches and rows of carts chained together, a method which many of them had learned in the French wars. Against this, on June 28th, King Richard dispatched the vanguard of his army, under his uncle, Thomas of Woodstock and Sir Thomas Percy, brother of the Earl of Northumberland. The few thousand rebels fought hard and tenaciously but were eventually overwhelmed by the superior forces of the King, comprising many mounted men and trained bands. The entrenchments were carried, the carts pulled to one side, and, in the fierce in-fighting that took place, the rebels were forced to retreat into the woods, leaving over five hundred dead on the field of battle.

One report states that the rebels were overcome by a surprise attack when sleeping. Doubtless they were tired, and suffering from the psychological shock of the London débacle, but nevertheless, they obviously fought well for the freedom they desired, as is evidenced by the heavy casualties they suffered.

The remnant, under John Ball, Adam Michel and John Kyrkeby, regrouped and fell back east towards Colchester, the town of their origin. Here, they hoped, they would find support in order to enable them to continue the fight. Within the hallowed walls of England's oldest town, they might yet be able to defy their pursuers.

CHAPTER 24

King Richard Enters Colchester

THE rebels arrived in Colchester towards the end of the month and found things somewhat different from those which prevailed three short weeks ago when they left the town to march on London. The enthusiasm of those days seemed to have vanished. Many of the merry men who joined the Revolt had now trickled back into the town, bringing with them news not only of the death of Wat Tyler, but also the report of the tragic rout at Billericay. There was an air of defeatism everywhere in the town. Men and women looked fearfully at one another, almost afraid to speculate on what might be going to happen. They all feared the forthcoming vengeance of the King. As one contemporary writer put it, "In London, Colchester men made a fine loud noise. Now, no one will admit that he was ever there!"

Consequently, when the defeated, dispirited remnant of the Billericay battle appealed to the town for help, the worthy burgesses, who had cheered so hard when they left the town, now did not want to know. Walsingham reports it in this fashion:–

> "Those rebels who had been scattered, reassembled once more and went to Colchester where they began to incite the townsmen by means of urgent entreaties, threats and arguments to yet new disturbances and madness. But, failing to do this, they moved on to Sudbury".[1]

It was at Sudbury that this last pathetic little band of survivors was attacked by a loyal force under Lord Fitz-Walter,

---

[1] Op. cit., pp. 21/22.

Lord of the Manor of Lexden, near Colchester, and Sir John Harleston. They were routed here, many captured, and the rest scattered to the winds. A few fled in another direction and tried to escape northwards towards Huntingdon. The burghers of this town also refused to help them and drove them off. The *Anonimalle Chronicle* reports:–

"Meanwhile, a party of the commons took their way towards Huntingdon in order to pass towards the north, where, in their malice and villany, they intended to ravage the land and destroy good men; but they were turned back and could not pass the bridge of that town because William Wightman, spigurnel of Chancery,[1] Walter of Rudham and other good men of the town of Huntingdon and the neighbouring country, met them on the bridge and gave them battle killing two or three of the commons. Therefore the rest were glad to fly and went to Ramsey in order to pass that way".[2]

At Ramsey, the rebels appealed to the Abbey for help, and the Abbot gave them bread, wine, ale and other victuals. Thoroughly exhausted, they lay down to sleep and were attacked by a gang of Huntingdon men who killed twenty-four of them, the others fleeing and eventually being hunted down in the surrounding countryside. For this loyal act, the men of Huntingdon received the King's thanks. It is reported that on 22nd May 1382, William Wightman was granted a royal pension of 6d daily for his services in repelling the commons at Huntingdon.[3] Rebel-bashing certainly paid off in those days!

There is no report of what happened to the leaders. It is possible that, as Colchester men, they fled back to that town, which Ball, at any rate, knew well. Michel and Kyrkeby were equally conversant with the local topography. All three went into hiding, fearful for the future.

Richard was now advancing slowly into Essex, engaged in his pacification of the county. On July 2nd he was in Chelmsford, issuing a proclamation formally revoking all the charters issued at Mile End, and setting up an Assize to deal

---

[1] A sealer of Chancery writs.
[2] Op. cit., pp. 150–1.
[3] C.P.R., 1381–5, p.120.

with captured rebels. He moved on to Colchester the same day, and again issued a formal revocation of all his promises. An Assize was set up here, under Sir Robert Tresilian, Chief Justice of Essex and Kent, who proceeded to deal sternly with this town which was the centre of the Revolt. Any Colchester men who were active in the rising were condemned to hanging, some to drawing and quartering in addition, which Sir Robert deemed to be a fitting punishment for those guilty of political crimes. His Assize became known as the 'Bloody Assize' and so many were sentenced to hanging by this severe judge that there was a shortage of gibbets in the town and carpenters to make them. Walsingham reports that nineteen men might be seen hanging from one beam.[1]

King Richard's continued emphasis, in his proclamations, of his disassociation from the charters he had previously granted, together with a denial, issued on June 23rd,[2] that the rebels were acting with his authority and wish, gives some credence to the belief that he had encouraged this insurrection. In Cambridge, the revolutionary leaders, in order to get the active support of the common people, had actually given out that they were acting on the command and at the wish of the King. And in Hertfordshire, we are even told that the Standard raised by the insurgents, was actually emblazoned with the King's arms.[3] When we consider the powerful position of the great Duke of Lancaster and Richard's hatred of him, it is not unreasonable to think that the latter might have been quite happy to have used the support of the people as a counterpoise to the influence of his uncle. To have him cut down to size would, undoubtedly, enhance his own royal popularity.

If Richard had been in communication with some of the rebels, it might throw a new light on several points which need elucidation. It would lend a fresh significance to the antagonism shown during the Revolt to the Duke of Lancaster, and to the way his agents were sought out and killed, and his manors destroyed, particularly in East Anglia. Also, if it had been rumoured that the King was overtly behind the Rising,

---

[1] Op. cit., p. 317.
[2] Assize Roll 103.m.1.
[3] Coram Rege Rolls, 482.Rex.16.

116

this might explain why so many of the country gentry gave their support. And it would be easier to understand, what has always been in need of explanation, namely, why the rebels transferred their allegiance so readily at Smithfield after the death of Wat Tyler. And, finally, we may now see why, if there was even a suspicion that the King was behind the movement, there was a hesitation on the part of those in authority in taking prompt measures to suppress it.

This may be only a theory, but Richard's continual assertion on important occasions, at Chelmsford, Colchester, and other towns, that he had no connection with the Rising, and wished to disown any previous part in it, or promise made to it, could make one think that "he protesteth too much". In view of his known character, it is doubtful if he could have worked out such a subterfuge on his own. But there were clever and experienced people behind him, like the Earl of Salisbury and his mother, the Princess Joan. These were capable of planning the Smithfield murder and would certainly not hesitate to execute any other devious plan to their advantage.

At any rate, Colchester on July 2nd, 1381, marked the final end of organised resistance by the people. Richard, standing before the Moot Hall in the High Street, surrounded by five hundred lancers and men-at-arms, told them firmly and unequivocally, where they stood. They were to remain serfs and villeins, as before – more so, if possible.

John Ball, Adam Michel, John Kyrkeby, hiding in the shadows of St. Runwald's Church opposite, and hearing the King's words, sped silently away, the two latter to the Essex marshes which they knew, and John Ball to the town of Coventry where he had friends.

CHAPTER 25

Disaster Everywhere

THE situation was now going from bad to worse for the rebels all over the surrounding countryside. In nearby Suffolk, the pacification of the county was a comparatively easy task. The Earl of Suffolk, William Ufford, marched on Bury St. Edmunds on June 23rd with five hundred lances. Confronted by this formidable force, Wrawe's rebel bands melted away, without making any great show of resistance. Wrawe himself fled into hiding, but was soon captured and brought to London for trial. In the course of this, he turned King's evidence, and drew up a long list implicating all his chief lieutenants. This contained facts about the way in which the risings in Suffolk spread northwards from the Essex border towards Bury St. Edmunds, and also a description of the methods he and his associates used in their plundering and blackmailing expeditions. Réville describes Wrawe as a bandit chief "ambitieux sans idées et cupide sans scruples". But the rebel's confession served him to little purpose, for he was hung, drawn and quartered like the others. He was one of the least creditable of the priest leaders of the Rising.

The Revolt in the rest of East Anglia was quelled by the determined action of Henry Despenser, Bishop of Norwich, one of the few of the nobility who showed any real presence of mind or active energy in dealing with it. This resolute young churchman, on whose head the helmet sat more naturally than the mitre, moved into action as soon as he heard about the rebellion. Issuing from his manor at Burleigh, with only eight lancers and a few archers, the normal retinue for a travelling prelate, he gathered recruits from the local gentry, and cut across to Peterborough, the Abbey of which had been occupied by the rebels. Taking them by surprise, he drove them out of the building and restored order in the town, small as his numbers were. Moving on to Ramsey, he destroyed a rebel force there, under Robert Tavell, one of Wrawe's lieutenants, on June 18th. He next proceeded to Cambridge, where, as we have seen, there was considerable disorder. Here, having gathered further support as he went along, (nothing succeeding as much as success), he subdued the rebellious town, executing John Hanchach and others in the Market Place. He dismissed the weak, compliant Mayor, Edmund Redmeadow, as "notoriously insufficient", and restored all the old privileges to the University. Staying in Cambridge for a couple of days on June 19th and 20th, he then moved via Newmarket to his own diocese. On the morning of the 22nd, at Temple Bridge, near Icklingham, on the Suffolk border, he ran into the embassy that Geoffrey Litster had dispatched south to obtain charters of manumission for Norfolk. The astute bishop, summing up the situation, released the two knights, Sir William Morley and Sir John Brewes, and promptly executed Litster's luckless lieutenants, Trunch, Skeet and Kybytt, by the wayside. He finally pressed on to his cathedral town, Norwich.

As soon as his approach was noised abroad, the gentry of both Western Suffolk and Norfolk, who had been in hiding, came out and flocked to his banner. As Walsingham reports:–

"All the knights and men of gentle blood who had hid themselves for fear of the commons, when they saw their bishop in helm and cuirass, girt with his two-edged sword, joined themselves to his company".[1]

On June 24th, Despenser was at the gates of Norwich, at the head of a considerable force.

Litster and the main rebel contingent had left the city on hearing of the bishop's advance. It is not known exactly why he went, possibly he feared to fight in the close confines of an urban area, and preferred to take up a defensive position in the open. In this he showed his lack of tactical skill, a weakness evidenced by most insurgent leaders with perhaps the exception of Tyler. They had not realised that their men would probably do better at in-fighting than in the traditional open battle.

---

[1] Op. cit., p. 306.

The 'King of the Commons' retreated to North Walsham where he sent urgent messages to all his supporters, urging them to rally round him and "strike to tame the malice of the bishop". He did not get as much support as he would have liked, as the news from London had been circulating for ten days now, and the recent report from Peterborough had doubtless come in. Nevertheless, he had gathered round him quite a numerous following behind a fortified position with a ditch and palisades, his flanks being covered by wagons chained wheel to wheel, and piles of furniture.

Bishop Despenser gave one look at this rather amateurish system of defences and decided on an immediate resolute charge. Leaping the ditch at the head of his knights, he burst through the palisades, and together they hurled themselves headlong upon the rebels. Litster's men stood firm and fought hard, but, eventually, the superior numbers and better weapons of the episcopal army prevailed, and the insurgents' line broke. Some escaped but many were slain and captured, including Litster. The Bishop, playing out his dual role, first as judge condemning the Norfolk leader to be hanged, drawn and quartered and then, relapsing into his clerical guise, he confessed and absolved the rebel himself. His final piece of medieval play-acting, occurring as the hapless rebel was being conveyed to the site of the execution, is described fittingly by Walsingham:—

> "The bishop himself, having heard and absolved his confession himself by virtue of his office, accompanied Littestere to the gallows, thereby performing, despite his victory, a work of mercy and pity. He held up the rebel's head to prevent it knocking on the ground while he was being dragged to the place of his hanging".[1]

In this fashion perished Geoffrey Litster, self-styled 'King of the Norfolk Commons', a man devoid of self-interest and devoted to the cause of the people. This 'immortal dyer' will remain an inspiration to many in that county of Norfolk where he lived, worked and died. His principal lieutenant, Sir Roger Bacon, was captured, imprisoned, fined and eventually

---

[1] Op. cit., p. 308.

released. He was fortunate in two respects; he was a knight, and he possessed the means to pay the fine.

When King Richard moved on to St. Albans on July 12th at the head of one thousand men, determined to have vengeance, there was very little opposition. In fact, neither the Abbot nor the tenants of the Abbey really wanted him to come, for, fearing his interference, they had managed to patch up their quarrel. But come the King did, with Sir Robert Tresilian for good measure. An Assize was set up, and a jury sworn in. A list of names of rebels deemed guilty was placed before them which they were compelled to accept. This was placed before a second jury who were asked if they could impugn the finding. Dutifully (and fearfully) they said NO. The same was done to a third jury, and the result was announced as a conviction by the unanimous verdict of thirty-six men!

The townsfolk of St. Albans were compelled to give up their charters and resume their position under the Abbot, and pay a fine of £200. About eighty people were arrested in the town, and the whole population was assembled in the great court of the Abbey, acknowledged their guilt, and swore never again to rise in arms. William Grindcobbe, their leader, was imprisoned to await trial. He was liberated on bail in the hope that he would use his influence with the citizens to procure their speedy submission. But, he was a disappointment to the Abbot and the authorities, for his speech to the people provides the most moving epitaph on the Revolt at St. Albans, even when produced from the not exactly sympathetic pen of his fellow monk, Walsingham:–

"Fellow citizens, for whom a little liberty has now relieved the long years of oppression, stand firm while you can and do not be afraid because of my persecution. For if it should happen that I die in the cause of seeking to acquire liberty, I will count myself happy to end my life as such a martyr".[1]

Grindcobbe the monk, a man of courageous bearing and attractive personality, returned to prison, and was hanged, drawn and quartered at St. Albans, on July 15th, a few hours

---

[1] Op. cit., pp. 299–301.

before his great leader and fellow priest, John Ball, suffered the same fate in the same place. Grindcobbe's friends in St. Albans stole away his body, and that of his fellow rebels in the town, and buried them. Their deed was discovered later, and they were compelled to dig up the bodies, now far gone in corruption, and hang them up again with their own hands.

The town of St. Albans returned to its previous ecclesiastical rule by Abbot de la Mare and his monks. But it had to wait until the Reformation before it was able to enjoy the liberty dreamed of by one of its Abbey's humble monks by the name of Grindcobbe.

CHAPTER 26

John Ball's Arrest, Trial and Execution

JOHN BALL was arrested, hiding in an old house in Coventry on July 13th. Perhaps some local citizen, fearful for his own position and desirous of gaining the approbation of the authorities, had betrayed the whereabouts of the wanted rebel leader, who was escorted immediately to St. Albans and arraigned before the infamous Chief Justice, Sir Robert Tresilian, at his Assize there. Ball faced his accusers fearlessly, and acknowledged taking a leading part in the Revolt. He admitted sending the letters inciting people to rebel, denied that his doings were blameworthy, and refused to ask for pardon.

It is interesting to note that Ball was not indicted for the murder of Archbishop Sudbury and the others, or even for conspiracy to murder. He was only indicted for making rebellion against the Crown, for inciting to rebellion, and for writing seditious letters. As the law stood at the time, only the first two mentioned should have been considered as capital offences. It would appear that he was give a jury trial, and that the jury acquitted him of every charge except that of writing the letters, which he had admitted doing.

Even so, Judge Tresilian, who usually condemned every rebel to death automatically, sentenced Ball to be hanged, drawn, quartered and beheaded. King Richard who was present at the trial, offered to use his royal prerogative and mitigate the sentence slightly by allowing the victim to hang until he was dead, a good deal less painful experience, if he would kneel to his King. Ball refused to do this.

He was being taken out immediately for execution when William Courtenay, Bishop of London, and shortly to be made Archbishop of Canterbury in the place of the murdered Sudbury, intervened, asking for a two days stay of execution to try to "save Ball's soul for the Church". This was granted by Sir Robert.

In the course of this postponement, Courtenay is alleged to have obtained a confession from John Ball. This is found in only one document, the remarkable *Fasciculi Zizaniorum,* written by a Carmelite monk towards the end of the fourteenth century. As a matter of interest, it is worth recording:—

> "When Balle realised he was doomed, he called to him William, Bishop of London and later of Canterbury, as well as lords Walter Lee, knight, and John Profete, notary; and he confessed publicly to them that for two years he had been a disciple of Wycliffe and had learned from the latter the heresies which he had taught; from Wycliffe had arisen the heresy concerning the sacrament of the altar and Balle had openly preached this and other matters taught by him. Balle also declared that there was a certain company of the sect and doctrines of Wycliffe which conspired like a secret fraternity and arranged to travel around the whole of England preaching the beliefs taught by Wycliffe: in this way it was planned that all England would consent at the same time to his perverse doctrine. Balle named to them Wycliffe himself as the principal author, and also mentioned Nicholas Hereford, John Aston and Laurence Bedenam, Masters of Arts. Balle added that if they had not encountered resistance to their plans, they would have destroyed the entire kingdom within two years".[1]

For reasons I have stated in Chapter 7, this 'confession' is, as R. B. Dobson says, an obvious fabrication. And Rodney Hilton adds that if anything of the kind had been true, we should have heard of it from contemporary sources. What makes this such an obvious invention is that the names mentioned place the whole thing so out of time. Nicholas

---

[1] *Fasciculi Zizaniorum.* Rolls Series, 1858, p. 273.

Hereford, John Aston and Laurence Bedenam were Lollard leaders, working with Wycliffe, who first came into prominence and got into trouble with the authorities in 1382, a year after the Revolt. They would be known to someone like the author of the *Fasciculi Zizaniorum*, writing towards the *end* of the century, and certainly *not* to Ball who, as we have said, was active for twenty years or more before Wycliffe and his Lollard associates came on the scene.

What is more likely to have happened during this brief stay of execution, as Lindsay and Groves suggest, is that Courtenay used it to try and obtain from Ball some information about the Great Society. The Bishop of London was a shrewd man, seeing already the prize of the now vacant Archbishopric coming into his hands, and any information he could obtain about Ball's associates, or bring further candidates for Sir Robert to condemn to the gallows, would stand him in good stead with the ruling class. Human lives were but cheap stepping stones to advancement in 1381.

An interesting similarity to note is that of the alleged confession of John Ball's fellow leader, Jack Straw, before he was executed in London. In return for Masses said for his soul, he is alleged to have revealed to Lord Mayor Walworth the rebel plans which included the arrest and execution of leading magnates and the seizure of all Church property. All bishops and higher clergy would be eliminated, leaving only the mendicant orders to carry on the administration of the Sacraments. Finally, the King himself would have been killed, and "when there was no one greater or stronger or more learned than ourselves surviving, we would have made such laws as pleased us".[1]

Most modern critics have rejected this story of Straw's confession, though Dobson thinks that some parts of it are not too 'implausible'. It is not so strange, perhaps, that two of the great leaders of the Revolt should both have 'phoney' confessions attributed to them, as contemporary writers had nothing but contempt and opprobrium to shower on anyone connected with the 1381 rising.

---

[1] *Chronicon Angliae*, pp. 309/10.

The chroniclers all report Ball's death briefly, without much comment. Not one of them suggests that he died anything but bravely. He was executed on the morning of Monday, July 15th, 1381, at Rome Lands, a public square near St. Albans Abbey, in the presence of King Richard and some of his ministers. With him died fifteen burgesses, small business men of St. Albans, who were guilty only of asking for charters of freedom. He was hung, drawn and quartered, and the four portions of his body were sent to hang in four different parts of the country, as an example to others who might have similar ideas of justice and freedom, and try to put them into practice.

CHAPTER 27

What Went Wrong?

THE sudden collapse of the first ever mass rising of the English people for freedom and justice, inevitably leads to the question being asked, Why did this happen? What went wrong? For it would appear that the rebels had everything on their side. Their cause was a just and righteous one. They were well organised and well led. There was a spiritual drive behind their movement. They were not mercenaries, intent on acquiring loot, but men who knew what they were fighting for, men who could echo the words of their leader, "We come not as thieves and robbers; we come seeking social justice".

Their opponents, the nobility of England and the hierarchy of the Church, on the other hand, were, admittedly, corrupt and inefficient. They were selfish and self-centred, concerned only with maintaining their own position of power and privilege. They had no interest in the welfare of the community as a whole. They lived, unashamedly, on the backs of the people.

It was the rebels who, in their proclamations, talked about the need to work for the common good, striving to remove all that would be harmful for the community in the future. They envisaged a nobility of all people alike, working and living in harmony under a just and fair ruler. They fought with the watchword in their hearts, 'With King Richard and the True Commons'.

And yet, as one historian has aptly put it, they failed when they were "within a dagger thrust of victory", when everything appeared to be going well for them. It might be interesting to consider possible reasons for this tragic failure.

First of all, the rebels possessed an amazing faith in the

person of royalty. They had a reverence for their King which was one of the most remarkable characteristics of the whole of the working class of that period. Their loyalty to him was unswerving, one of the truly almost inexplicable aberrations which proved to be a major factor in deciding the issue of the Revolt. King Richard, the rebels thought, was with them. As a King, he must rule in the interests of all the people. He stood above the intrigues and evil doings of the nobles, was untainted by the corruption of his ministers, and, possessing the supreme power, it was he alone who would really help his humble subjects. It was to the King they must appeal, and this was one of the prime objects of their march on London.

The insurgents had a two-fold purpose in approaching their King. One was, of course, to obtain redress from him for the hardships they were suffering as serfs and villeins. They desired only to live in the future as free men and women, able to hold up their heads with dignity. They wanted, simply, freedom and justice for all. And, secondly, they had realised that their King was an inexperienced boy, who might need help. They were coming to pledge their support for him, by removing the collection of evil, self-seeking ministers and nobles who surrounded him. Then, he would be free to rule for all.

This was the great illusion which coloured the thinking of the insurgents and their leaders, and which was to inhibit and thwart their ultimate purpose. They did not know the true situation which was that King Richard, like all the monarchs who preceded and succeeded him, was never on the side of the people, but merely a representative of the Establishment of his day.

Another point which the rebels failed to take into account was the duplicity of their opponents. They had not realised how determined the ruling classes were to continue to hold on to their position of power. There was nothing these would not do in its defence, no action they would not take to maintain it, and no low trick they would not stoop to perpetrate, if it were threatened. Although the rebels had suffered all their lives under the oppression of their rulers, they were still unable to appreciate that these were ruthless men who would stick at nothing to defend their status. To defeat the insurgents, the nobility felt thay had a divine right to use any methods.

The insurgents did not appreciate this, still assuming that it was a small group of corrupt ministers and nobles who were at fault, and that most of the aristocracy were reasonable people. Thus, there is no evidence that there was any attack on the gentry as a class, during the Revolt; only the known evil ones were dealt with. The 'gentlemen' were never a prime target.

The fact that some of the nobility did side with the rebels was not exactly helpful for their cause. For these men were but transient comrades in their camp, as it turned out. For, strange to relate, in all the cases of the knights, wealthy squires and business men who joined the insurgents, not one is reported to have been executed. All were fined and pardoned, returning to the natural fold of their class with alacrity. What John Ball, Wat Tyler and the other leaders did not understand, when they welcomed these knights and squires into their ranks, was what modern sociologists have now pointed out, namely, that whoever attempts to seize power, or even seizes power in any country, it is the old 'Establishment' which will continue to rule.

Karl Marx postulated that history had proved that no ruling group ever gave up its power voluntarily, but only after a bitter struggle. And, it was a British Prime Minister, one Stanley Baldwin, who once said that whatever party came into office, it was the Conservatives who would always be in power. Britain today is, in actual fact, ruled by the 'established' civil servants, and will continue to be so, come what may.

A further reason for the rebel failure was an underlying feeling of inferiority and insecurity, which expressed itself at times. In spite of their growing consciousness of class solidarity, they were still influenced by their immediate past. Thus, when at Smithfield, they were tricked by King Richard into proceeding to the Clerkenwell Fields, and found Sir Robert Knolles awaiting them there with the London trained bands, they offered no resistance. Hearing Sir Robert call out, "Fall out you wretches! Slack your bowstrings and be gone!",[1] they obeyed like a flock of sheep. They could have easily fought back, and possibly have won the day, even then, for they were well

---

[1] *Eulogium Historiarum*, III, p. 354.

armed, in battle array, and still had some good leaders. But, they were what feudalism had made them, conditioned to obey authority, and, when confronted by armed forces and overlords, their old fear and servility rose and submerged them.

An important and vital flaw in the character of Wat Tyler had what could be called a decisive effect on the course of the Revolt. This was his action and behaviour when confronting the King and his party at Smithfield. It seems inconceivable that a man with Wat's military experience should have been so stupid as to ride out, away from his own army, accompanied by one supporter only carrying his banner, and go right into the midst of an armed group of his opponents. This was sheer suicide, and his loss as a leader undoubtedly decided the future of the Revolt.

It is possible that, flushed with the thought of victory now within his grasp, he had relaxed his usual caution. The *Anonimalle* alone reports this incident of Tyler calling for a jug of water, rinsing his mouth with it and then spitting it out rudely, followed by "a great draught" from a jug of ale. After this, he clambered on his horse and, before he could ride away, was attacked.[1] The strong ale may have gone to his head and rendered him less than alert, but he could not have known that his opponents were armed, as they had all concealed their weapons. It is not easy to come to a verdict.

R. B. Dobson, in his introduction, sums it up in this fashion:–
"The differing accounts of Tyler's death at Smithfield can probably never be satisfactorily reconciled. All the evidence has undergone some distortion, and it is impossible to substantiate in full either of the two most ingenious interpretations:– that Tyler was the innocent victim of a pre-conceived royalist plot, or that he truculently provoked a violent reaction from the royal party in order to restore his waning authority over his men".[2]

The murder of their great leader, followed by a hopelessly and deliberately confused situation, was too much for the rebels

---

[1] Op. cit., pp. 140/150.
[2] Op. cit., p. 25.

to cope with. They were unprepared for this sort of cunning from opponents who, they had never realised, were always one jump ahead of them.

CHAPTER 28

The Peasants' Revolt in the Folk Tradition

THE effect of the Peasants' Revolt on the subsequent development in England is not easy to assess. First of all, historians are not agreed as to what it achieved. Some say that it had very little effect, and that things went on more or less the same for a time. Others insist that the Revolt was responsible for major changes in the relationships between the nobles and the serfs. R. B. Dobson, for example, expresses the view that, in, general, the results of the great Revolt seem to have been negative where they were not negligible. Rodney Hilton, after stating that the case is as difficult to prove as to disprove, would appear to agree with this when he affirms that the most ambitious of the mass movements of peasants were undoubtedly failures as far as the full achievement of their aims was concerned. He does, however, admit that some limited peasant aims were achieved. Lindsay and Groves maintain that, although conditions of serfdom were worse immediately after the Revolt, it did mark the beginning of a social revolution. In this latter view, they are supported by Anthony Steel in his *Richard II.*[1] Oman sums it all up by stating that the great rebellion of 1381 does not mark the end, any more than it marks the beginning, of the struggle between the landholder and the peasant.

There were, of course, other revolts which broke out subsequently to 1381, notably that of Jack Cade in Kent, in 1450, and Robert Kett in Norfolk in 1549, both similar to the original Peasants' Revolt in methods and aims. So, as late as the

---

[1] C.U.P. 1962.

summer of 1549, nearly two hundred years on, we find the Norfolk rebels demanding "that all bond men may be free, for God made all free with his precious blood shedding", almost re-echoing the sentiments of John Ball's sermon.[1]

But, there was one area in which the Peasants' Revolt did seem to have some immediate impact, and this was in the religio-political sphere. For the Lollard movement under Wycliffe received a great impetus from the year 1382 onwards when it first began to have some growth, as referred to in Chapter 7. And this impetus, carrying on into the following century, with two great risings of its own, was derived from the continuing 1381 spirit and should be credited to John Ball rather than John Wycliffe.

However, in the folk tradition, the Peasants' Revolt, for several centuries to come, came to be looked upon as a result of man's sinfulness and God's consequent displeasure, a sort of divine retribution for having dared to challenge a divinely ordered system. Conservative publicists were quick to spread the argument that unchecked religious dissent and heresy would eventually cause the collapse of the social order and possibly bring about conditions similar to those of the dreaded 'Hurling Time'. This soon became an accepted way of thinking about 1381.

Even after the Reformation, the Revolt survived in folk memory as the classic example of the fate that would happen to a country where the natural principles of class division collapsed, and order was replaced by chaos. From the late fourteenth to the late eighteenth centuries, the rights and wrongs of the actions of John Ball, Wat Tyler and the other leaders of the Revolt, were never given serious consideration. Disobedience to those in authority, the nobles and the nobles' servants, was the paramount issue. This must be avoided as mortal sin. This theme, "O Lord, how horrible a thing is division in a realm!", is found in both early and late Elizabethan drama. *The Life and Death of Jack Strawe*, [2] a play published in 1593, is an example of this, though it does present

---

[1] A. Fletcher, *Tudor Rebellions*, pp. 74.143.
[2] *Old English Drama*, Students' Facsimile Edition, 1911.

the rebels and their grievances with a certain amount of sympathy.

Even in the days of the English republic, in the mid-seventeenth century, there was still no sympathy felt for the 1381 rebels. In *The Rustick Rampant*, the first detailed history of the Revolt, written by John Cleveland, a cavalier poet, we find these words put into the mouth of Richard II, "The world cannot subsist without Order and Subjection, men cannot be freed from Lawes".[1] And, one of the greatest of the Levellers, John Lilburne, regarded men like Wat Tyler and Jack Straw as "contemners of Authority" rather than seeing them as those who belonged to their own revolutionary tradition.

It was only after the outbreak of the French Revolution in 1789, that John Ball and Wat Tyler began to come into their own in the English folk tradition, enjoy posthumous recognition as spokesmen for the poor and disinherited, and become looked upon as true apostles of popular liberty. Since the age of Elizabethan drama, the Peasants' Revolt had always been a subject of popular entertainment because of its inherent dramatic interest. But only towards the end of the eighteenth century did Ball and Tyler appear in the popular mind as England's first revolutionary leaders. Both appeared in the famous battle of words between Edmund Burke and Thomas Paine which ensured that the rebels of 1381 were now fairly established as founding-fathers of the English radical movement. Both Burke and Paine were the first writers to attempt to show the relevance of Ball and Tyler to the modern world. Burke, in *An Appeal From the New to the Old Whigs*,[2] with heavy sarcasm compares the Peasants' Revolt to the French Revolution, while Paine in, *The Rights of Man*,[3] takes up his cudgel in defence of the rebels, and pays a great tribute to Wat Tyler, describing him as "an intrepid, disinterested man with respect to himself". He concludes, "If the Barons merited a monument to be erected in Runnymede, Tyler merits one in Smithfield".

Later, we have the poet, Robert Southey, who found the

---

[1] J. Cleveland, *The Rustic Rampant*, (London 1658), p. 65.

[2] Oxford *World Classics 1907*, v. 102–4.

[3] Everyman Ed. 1915, pp. 236/7.

theme of the Peasants' Revolt irresistible, publishing in 1817, a dramatic poem entitled *Wat Tyler,*[1] a work quite as revolutionary in tone as the more famous works of Byron and Shelley. About this time the Chartists were active, proudly naming one of their groups 'The Wat Tyler Brigade'. The Sheffield Chartists in the 1840's painted portraits of their heroes, ranging from Wat Tyler to Byron and Shelley, on their home-made banners, which, alas, have not survived. There is a record also of one self-appointed, political descendent of Wat Tyler in the person of Bradford Chartist, Isaac Jefferson, 'alias Wat Tyler', a man of herculean strength who aroused consternation in 1848. A Chartist song of the period had the words:–

"For Tyler of old,
A heart-chorus bold,
Let Labour's children sing."

Finally, towards the end of the century, we have William Morris producing his *Dream of John Ball,*[2] in which he voices the aspirations of the 1381 rebels in idealistic fashion, marred only by the typical sentimentality of approach of the age in which he lived.

Very little in the way of tangible memorial of the Revolt remains with us today. There is a stone cross beside the road from North Walsham to Norwich which is said to mark the field of the battle there in 1381. And, in the Fishmongers Hall in London, a wooden effigy of Mayor Walworth is to be found, together with the dagger with which he is said to have stabbed Wat Tyler. Also the skull of Archbishop Simon of Sudbury may be inspected in St. Gregory's Church in that town, near which, in recent years, a number of graves with headless skeletons were found, a grim reminder of the fate of local rebels.

It has been said that very few of the revolutionary or 'left-wing' British parties in more recent times have ever taken the rebels of 1381 very warmly to their hearts. This may be due to the lack of accurate information about the insurgents and their motives. It must be admitted that Tyler, Ball and company

---

[1] W. T. Sheraton (London 1819).
[2] Morris, Selected Works, ed. E. D. H. Cole (Nonesuch Press, 1948).

have not had much of an image presented by the media. It is hardly in the interests of an Establishment-controlled Press, radio or television, to praise a revolt, the chief aim of which was the destruction of the Established Order of its day. So, our revolutionaries have not had a very good Press.

However, on occasions, something does come through. It was perhaps startling, a few years back, at an Old Bailey Trial of a young Doctor of Philosophy, to hear her declaim in her defence the imperishable words of Wat Tyler – "We come not as thieves and robbers, we come seeking social justice!".

It is not possibly known to many but there are at least two churches where John Ball, the Revolt inspirer and leader, is remembered. In the beautiful medieval church of Thaxted in Essex, there is a small altar erected to his memory, and at Holy Trinity Church, Dalston, in London, a memorial service was held there on July 15th each year in honour of the rebel martyr, at which, on occasions, I myself have taken part.

Until latterly, visitors to England often remarked that there appear to be no commemorative plaques anywhere to those who took part in the Peasants' Revolt, with the exception of Walworth and Farringdon who have streets name after them.[1] In West Smithfield, where the decisive events took place, there are plaques to Protestant martyrs and a 'Scottish Nationalist', but no visible memorial to one of the greatest rebels of them all, Wat Tyler. In his home town of Colchester, where he and his comrade-in-arms, John Ball, planned it all, their names were unknown, even to some of its more enlightened citizens. But this has recently changed. For Colchester Borough Council, in response to representations made by myself, has now named two footpaths, in their new housing estate in the old Dutch Quarter of the town, after John Ball and Wat Tyler. One of these, named after Ball, is practically on the site of the tenement he inherited from his deceased father in 1350, at the age of nineteen.

So, Ball and Tyler are now commemorated in the town of their origin, just as Robert Kett has been in his home city of

---

[1] Jack Straw's Castle, an inn on Hampstead Heath, London, dating back to the 1380's, is reputedly named after the rebel leader.

Norwich. These prophets will now not be without honour in their own country.

A most interesting trans-Atlantic connection has been discovered. In August, 1977, *Debrett's Peerage* declared that the roots of President Jimmy Carter, of the United States of America, go back to 1361, and have been traced to Jefferies Farm, Chipperfield, in Hertfordshire. One of his ancestors named John Carter, who lived in this farm, died in 1588, and there is a memorial to him in nearby King's Langley parish church. Further investigations have revealed records which show that an ancestor of this man, also a John Carter, was active in Hertfordshire during the Peasants' Revolt.

On July 15th, 1981, the six hundredth anniversary of his death, a fitting tribute to John Ball was established in Colchester's Dutch Quarter when a plaque to his memory was erected by the Museum Service, on behalf of Colchester Borough Council, close to where his father's cottage once stood.

CHAPTER 29

The Lesson of 1381 for Today

WHAT lessons are to be learned from a study of the Peasants' Revolt? A superficial reading of the events of 1381 would lead to the obvious answer that one thing we do learn from them is contained in the words of the Psalmist, "Put not thy trust in Princes!" Certainly the deviousness of royalty has never been better exposed than in the person of King Richard II. As the rebels found to their cost, it is never safe to give too much adulation to one particular regal person, or to place too much trust in him or her. For this has the effect of isolating the monarch, and, in isolation he or she will tend to become careless of popular feeling. A good King or Queen should possess, and continue to possess, the common touch. King Richard, brought up in the rarefied and unhealthily perverted atmosphere of his fourteenth century Court, never understood, or wanted to understand, the needs of his people. No thought of "noblesse oblige" ever entered his head, or the heads of the selfish ministers around him. The Crown was his by divine right, to be used and exploited as he wished.

Another fact which can be learned from the 1381 happenings, is the significance of the ease by which the common folk were manipulated by their rulers. This is a danger which applies to all societies at all times. King Richard's astute ministers knew that the large forces of the people could be defeated and controlled by superior cunning, and all that was necessary was to instil into the minds of the peasants the idea that the running of a country was a complicated business which only those with superior knowledge and education could tackle.

This inferiority complex has been dinned into the minds of the working people by their rulers from time immemorial, and persists to the present day. In my own experience, I found this to be so in a Suffolk country parish, where I could never get farm workers to come on the Church Council. It was 'them', (i.e. the squire, the parson, the doctor, and the wealthy farmers), who always ran things in the village, workers told me, not the likes of 'us'. Similarly, and on a larger scale, when the possibility of Britain entering the European Economic Community was being canvassed, Lord Macleod of Fiunary, wishing to know more about the issues, wrote to his Member of Parliament asking for information about the Treaty of Rome. The reply he got was that the said Treaty had not been published in English and, anyhow, it was far too complicated for the ordinary person to understand! It must be left to those in the know to work things out, presumably.

So, despite the efforts of John Ball, Wat Tyler and other leaders in 1381, there still persisted this domination by 'manipulation' of the people. Writing five hundred years after the Revolt, about the conditions of the nineteenth century agricultural labourer, (the descendants of the rebels of 1381), J. E. Thorold Rogers stated:

"Scattered and incapable of combined action with his fellows, bowed down by centuries of oppression, hard usage and hard words, with every social force against him, the landlords in league with the farmers, and the clergymen in league with both, the latter constantly preaching resignation, the two former constantly enforcing it, he has lived through evil times".[1]

Commenting on this, Rodney Hilton remarks:–

"This was not the immediate legacy of the defeat of the rebels in 1381, for the English peasants and artisans kept their end up against the landowner and employer, with varying success, for many years afterwards. But it was the ultimate legacy of the failure of the specific battle for freedom and for the end of villeinage. The noticeable tendency of the English to be self-congratulatory about

---

[1] *Six Centuries of Work and Wages*, 1903, p. 509.

having given the idea of liberty to the world with Magna Carta, could well be modified in the light not merely of the exclusion from its enjoyment of the mass of the population, but of the long-term consequences of that exclusion".[1]

But, in spite of these deadening long-term consequences of exclusion from the fruits of liberty, men have gone on fighting for it. The essentially antagonistic nature of the lord-peasant relationship was, and is, a continuing factor, the eternal struggle between the haves and the have-nots, or as a nineteenth century sociologist has put it, between those who own the means of production and those who do not. This is not something that was unique to the Peasants' Revolt of 1381, and John Ball's preaching and teaching was by no means exceptional but rather representative of a long established folk tradition, struggling for expression. In a paper delivered to the Anglo-Soviet Conference of Historians in September 1969, Rodney Hilton cites the case of the twelfth century poet Wace who ascribed to the rebellious Norman peasants in the year 996, the sentiment, "We are men like them . . . we can suffer like them!".

In the 1380's, as Hilton and Fagan have emphasised, "All conditions for an uprising were ripe", and John Ball certainly thought so with the reiteration in his letters of the warning, "Now is the time!". In his modern analysis of his own contemporary situation, Karl Marx pointed out that certain conditions must be present before any successful revolution can take place, namely, that there must be a great gap between the rich and the poor, the people must develop a class consciousness and themselves desire a change. These conditions would appear to be fulfilled in 1381 when, as a chronicler reported, "The people are in such a plight that they can give no more. I suspect that, if they had a leader, they would revolt". Surely, this was, in the words of Shakespeare, the tide in the affairs of men which, taken at its flood, must lead to victory.

But history seems to have indicated that although the Peasant's Revolt was necessary to start things off, it had to be

---

[1] Op. cit., p. 232.

followed by a lengthy process of slow economic changes before the desired result would come into being. The rebels were like the primers of the pump, the flux, the catalyst, which gave the necessary stimulus to the onward march of economic forces, forces such as the Black Death which was not of their making but contributed to the pattern they were beginning to weave.

Is this the way things must always happen, or can the result be achieved by a quick, violent, successful revolution as in some countries today? Could this be applicable to our modern, technological age? The question is worth considering.

Of course, conditions are somewhat different now. We don't have domination or manipulation by kings, lords or nobles. We have a democratic form of government. The people have their say in the running of the country. "It could never happen here", we say confidently when we think of the Hurling Time of 1381 (if we ever do). But further thinking might cause us to have a few doubts. For today we are beginning to find ourselves controlled by, and at the mercy of, groups more determined, more ruthless, more callous, and more insensitive to the needs of the people, than the whole long line of the Kings and Queens of England put together. These small controlling groups are the big monopolies and multi-nationals, who, by their manipulations can destroy the economic life of a nation overnight. They are of such magnitude and controlled by so few people, that they are very difficult to deal with. It's all a matter of degree. The lord-peasant relationship of the feudal system was followed by the squire-labourer relationship of the last few centuries, now replaced, in our largely urban life, by the monopoly-multinational-people relationship. In our much vaunted 'property owning democracy', 84% of the wealth of the country is still owned by 7% of the people.

Whether, in the Soviet Union, China, and the Eastern Democracies, where there are no private monopolies, they have managed to solve this problem is not easy to acertain. They are still very largely in a transitional period. Time will have to elapse before we can see the effect of slow economic forces on their experimenting. They had their revolutions quickly and pushed them to their ultimate conclusion without waiting for these economic forces to function. Like young men in a hurry, they pressed on regardless.

But for both them and us, John Ball's sermon, preached on Blackheath Common on June 13, 1381, is still the most moving plea for social equality in the history of the English language. When we look back across the more than six centuries that separate us from those portentous happenings, when the common folk of England, living under intolerable conditions, first rose in defence of their freedom, we must feel some sympathy for the ideals they held and the way they died for them. Although their brave attempt was frustrated and the Rising eventually crushed, their efforts mark one of the most important epochs in our history.

Writing at the end of the last century, Edgar Powell sums up the Peasants' Revolt in this way:—

> "It emphasised to the country at large, in a way there was no possiblity of mistaking, the fact that the working classes had arrived in a position of great power, and though, perhaps in disclosing that power, they had also disclosed their inability, as yet, to use it to the greatest effect, yet their strength and position had been shown to be such as no rulers could with safety ignore".[1]

Rodney Hilton, at the conclusion of one of his latest books, poses and answers the question we have been discussing, in this way:—

> "What could the fate of peasant societies in the present world of almost world-wide commercial and industrial monoploy capitalism have in common with that of the peasant societies of the late medieval world? Clearly, the tasks of leadership in contemporary peasant society have nothing in common with the tasks of the past, except in *the recognition that conflict is part of existence and that nothing is gained without struggle*".[2]

In one of his letters, John Ball wrote, "At the even, men heareth the day". In those Dark Ages, in the evening of English life, when the lights seemed to be dimming everywhere, there were those who heard the day, who had the vision of the

---

[1] Op. cit., p. 66.
[2] Op. cit., p. 236. Italics mine.

England of the future when men and women could live in happiness and freedom.

We have heard that day in our time, a day that is coming to pass, but one which was seen clearly, over six hundred years ago, by a humble parish chaplain in the Essex town of Colchester. He was, indeed, a true rebel before his time.

APPENDIX I

John Ball appears to have disregarded his early excommunication in 1364 by Simon of Sudbury, Bishop of London. For in 1366/67, Simon de Langham, Archbishop of Canterbury, cited Ball to appear before him and forbade anybody in the Deanery of Bocking to attend his sermons, as indicated in the following extract:–

"AGAINST JOHN BALL AND HIS ADHERENTS

"Simon, etc., to the Dean of Bocking, within our direct jurisdiction, and to and sundry rectors, vicars, and parochial chaplains of the said deanery, greeting. It has come to our attention, as a matter of notoriety, that a certain so-called priest, John Ball, is preaching within the above-mentioned area of our jurisdiction, many erroneous and scandalous things, both at the expense of the safety of his soul and the souls of his supporters, and to the manifest scandal of the universal church.

"We cannot of course tolerate such things with a clear conscience, and so we strictly commend each and all of you to issue a clear warning, in due form of law, to all and sundry persons within the said Deanery, strictly forbidding them to have anything to do with the preaching of the said John, on pains of excommunication, which will be automatically incurred by anyone who fails to obey the above-mentioned warnings. If you should discover offenders in this matter, you should cite them or make sure that they are cited to appear before us, on a given day of which you shall notify them, wherever we may then be, in our city, diocese or province of Canterbury.

"Moreover, you should cite or cause to be cited, the said John Ball to appear personally before us on a given day of which you shall notify him, to answer truthfully to certain articles and questions put to him by us by virtue of our office, touching the correction and safety of his soul and to obey the law in all respects. And you shall certify to us what you have done in these

matters, on the day and at the place aforesaid, by your letters patent, containing the names of those cited.
Dated 28 January 1366/67"

Langham's Register f.52. Printed in Wilkins *Concilia*, Vol. III, p. 64.

APPENDIX II

ORDER FOR JOHN BALL'S ARREST
ADDRESSED TO COLCHESTER CLERGY, 1376

"Commission to Robert Adewyne, parson of the church of Pantfield, Reynold, parson of the church of Little Teye, Thomas Joye of Colchestre, John Blyton of Colchestre and John Flecham of Shaldeford, to take John Balle, chaplain, who for his manifest contumacy has been excommunicated by authority of Simon, archbishop of Canterbury, as the latter has signified to the King by letters patent, and deliver him by indenture to the Sheriff of ESSEX, to compel him by his body according to the custom of England until Holy Church be satisfied in respect of his contempt and the injury done by him to her."
[*Cal. Pat. Roll*, 1374–77, p. 415. (sub. 1376)]

NOTE:
A strange coincidence occurs in connection with this. For John Blyton, of Colchester, appears on June 13th, 1381, as a royal envoy to the rebels at Blackheath to warn them not to approach London. He encounters Alderman Horne and his companions, also riding to contact the rebel force, and offers to join them, an offer which was refused. Blyton then delivers his own message to the insurgents, which was subsequently contradicted by Horne who invites them into the city.
[See, *Coram Rege Roll*, Easter 6 Richard II, (KB27/488) Rex.memb.6]

Three years later, we find John Blyton in prison at Corfe Castle in June 1384, and, five months later, released on the surety of John, Abbot of Colchester (*Cal. Close Rolls*, 7 Richard II, p. 369; 8 Richard II, pp. 470, 477, 596).

And, again a coincidence, the Abbot of St. John's Abbey, Colchester, from 1349–53 and from 1358–68, was a certain Simon de Blyton, presumably a relative of John Blyton.

APPENDIX III

COLCHESTER RED PAPER BOOK
(one of the oldest of Borough Archives, dated 1310, Trans. Gurney Benham, 1902) p. 156

ENTRY RESPECTING WAT TYLER'S REBELLION
Dorse of Folio 369(257) Latin (about ten lines lost by decay)

They took (ceperunt) ....
the same King, but ....
men from the more worthy persons of ....
they killed, and ....
Clerkenwell ....
they [burnt] and their goods and chattels ...... mercy,
...... Suffolk, on the day aforesaid ...... [Sir] John
Cavendish (?) (Johannem Cauen)...... in England, the prior
of the monastery of St. Edmund[1] ...... Cok a worthy man,
and a man of wealth in the same [county?] ...... and they
killed and beheaded ...... of which fury and treachery
(prodicionis) ...... Sudbery, chaplain,[2] was the chief cause to
whom ...... because a certain subsidy of twelve pence [was
levied on all persons], as well males as females, in England, of
the age of 15 years and upward, so that ...... they might have
helped ...... in the King's Parliament at L[ondon] on the
Monday following All Saints day in the fifth year of his reign
(1381) ...... And the said insurrection lasted throughout
three ...... and then the lords, chief magistrates (pretoribus)
magnates, and ...... being brought together (coordinatis)
...... with the King aforesaid, who caused those who had
incited (persons) against the said subsidy, to be hanged. But
afterwards ...... the King, by the advice of his parliament
granted grace to the said men ...... and pardoned them their
insurrection and treasons aforesaid. That thing is brought to
light (istud prefertur). Michael Aunger, Clerk of the Town of
Colchester, had made and written ...... [this record?]

...... with the utmost grief (maximo dolore), and .... "

(End of Dorse Folio 369 (257))

GURNEY BENHAM'S NOTES

[1] In Suffolk (A.D. 1381) the insurgents beheaded the Prior of Bury and Sir John Cavendish, the King's Chief Justice. *Eulogium Historiarum.*

[2] 'Sudbury capellanus'. Perhaps a mistake for 'cancellarius', i.e. Simon Sudbury, Archbishop and Chancellor, beheaded by the mob in London, June 14th, 1381.

MY NOTE

The late Mr Benham may have been mistaken here. 'Sudbury capellanus' could indeed be correct and mean 'Sudbury chaplain', referring to Thomas, chaplain at All Saints' Church, Sudbury, who was actively involved in the Rising in Suffolk.

APPENDIX IV

SELECT BIBLIOGRAPHY

LITERARY SOURCES

The Vision of William Concerning Piers the Plowman, by William Langland, edited by the Reverend Walter W. Skeat (Oxford University Press, 1893).

The Vision of Piers Plowman, by William Langland, translated by Henry W. Wells (Sheed and Ward, 1935. Reprinted 1959).

A Dream of John Ball (Stories in Prose), by William Morris, edited by G. D. H. Cole (Nonesuch Press, London, 1934).

HISTORIES

The Peoples History of Essex, by D. W. Coller (Meggy & Chalk, Chelmsford, 1861).

Lives of English Popular Leaders in the Middle Ages – No. 2: Tyler, Ball and Oldcastle, by C. E. Maurice (Henry S. King & Co., London, 1875).

Essex in Insurrection, 1381, 'Transactions of Essex Archaeological Society', by J. S. Sparvel-Bayly (Colchester, 1878).

The Rising in East Anglia in 1381, by Edgar Powell (Cambridge University Press, 1896).

England in the Age of Wycliffe, by G. M. Trevelyan (Longman 1899. Paperback 1972).

Studies in the Sources of the Social Revolt in 1381, by G. Kriehn (American Historical Review, VII, 1901–02).

The Great Revolt of 1381, by Charles Oman (Oxford University Press, 1906, reprinted 1969).

Genesis of Lancaster – Vol. 2, by James Ramsay (Oxford University Press, 1913).

The Peasants' Revolt of 1381, by Philip Lindsay and Reg. Groves (Hutchinson, 1950).

The English Rising of 1381, by R. H. Hilton and H. Fagan (Lawrence & Wishart, 1950).

Richard II, by Anthony Steel (Cambridge University Press, 1962).

Chaucer in His Time, by Derek Brewer (Thomas Nelson & Sons, 1963).

Lady of the Sun (The Life and Times of Alice Perrers), by F. George Kay (Frederick Muller, 1966).

English Historical Documents – Vol. IV, 1327–1485, edited by A. R. Myers (Eyre and Spottiswoode, 1969).

The Peasants' Revolt of 1381, by R. B. Dobson (Macmillan, 1970).

The Black Death and The Peasants' Revolt, by Leonard W. Cowie (Wayland Publishers, London, 1972).

Bond Men Made Free, by Rodney Hilton (Temple Smith, London, 1973).

The English Rebels, by Charles Poulsen (Journeyman Press, 1984).

NOVELS

Long Will, by Florence Converse (J. M. Dent & Sons, 1908, reprinted 1948).

English Episode, by Charles Poulsen (Progress Publishing Co., 1946).

Thunder on Saturday, by William Woods (Andrew Melrose, 1952).

The Golden Cage, by Philip Lindsay (Robert Hale, 1961. Reprinted Hutchinson Library Series, 1973).

Who Was Then The Gentleman?, by Charles E. Israel (Macmillan, 1963).

The Earthworms, by Prudence Andrew (Hutchinson, 1963).

The Immortal Dyer, by Neil Bell (Alvin Redman, 1964).

Swords Over Southdowne, by Harold Priestley (Frederick Muller, 1964).

Cry God For Glendower, by Martha Rofheart (Talmy, Franklin, 1973).

A Summer Storm, by Jane Lane (Peter Davies, 1976).

INDEX

151